主办单位　Hosted by
中华世纪坛世界艺术馆　Beijing World Art Museum
福建博物院　Fujian Museum
广州博物馆　Guangzhou Museum
东莞展览馆　Dongguan Exhibition Center
维尔康姆图书馆　Wellcome Library
嘉信文化　Credential International Arts Management

协办单位　Co-organized by
中国摄影出版社　China Photographic Publishing House

支持单位　Supported by
wellcome trust
歌华集团
BEIJING GEHUA CULTURAL CENTRE CO., LTD.
北京歌华文化发展集团

004 序一 / 王立梅，中华世纪坛世界艺术馆馆长
Foreword 1 / Wang Limei, Beijing World Art Museum
005 序二 / 杨琮，福建博物院院长
Foreword 2 / Yang Cong, Fujian Museum
006 序三 / 程存洁，广州博物馆馆长
Foreword 3 / Cheng Cunjie, Guangzhou Museum
007 序四 / 钟长永，东莞展览馆馆长
Foreword 4 / Zhong Changyong, Dongguan Exhibition Center

008 人类的汤姆逊 / 仝冰雪
John Thomson: A Humanist View of the World / Tong Bingxue

014 约翰·汤姆逊：从伦敦到中国，从中国到伦敦 / 威廉·舒巴赫，维尔康姆图书馆
John Thomson: London to China, China to London / William Schupbach, Wellcome Library

016 汤姆逊的中国照片和维尔康姆图书馆 / 周迅
Thomson's China Photographs and the Wellcome Library / Zhou Xun

018 图版
Plates

166 后记 / 姚詠蓓，嘉信文化
Postscript / Betty Yao, Credential International Arts Management

中华世纪坛世界艺术馆
2009年4月16日-5月18日

Beijing World Art Museum
16 April-18 May 2009

序　一

100多年前，当西方人用坚船利炮强行敲开中国大门的时候，出现在他们眼前的不仅有梦寐以求的广袤的原料产地、劳务市场和商品输出地，更有令他们无比震惊的古老中国在过去数千年时间里孕育并积淀下来的深厚历史和文化。于是，在武力的开道下，随着西洋商品一同涌入的也有不少对这个神秘国度文化的探访者，苏格兰摄影师约翰·汤姆逊无疑正是其中特别突出的一位。

汤姆逊被誉为纪实摄影的先驱之一。这不仅是因为他到达了包括中国在内的亚洲很多国家和地区，甚至深入到从没有外国人涉足过的中国内地，而且还源于他在中国人普遍对摄影尚一无所知的时代，凭借其良好的沟通能力，拍摄到了上至王公贵族，下至平民百姓等各个阶层，各个地方的风土人情。更为重要的是，相对于晚清其他造访中国的摄影师来说，汤姆逊的镜头是不带有民族偏见的，是最为客观、真实地反映其所见所闻的。除此之外，汤姆逊在回到英国后，又不遗余力地通过各类出版物，将这些中国照片广泛地介绍给西方人，充当了一个在当时少有的公正且纯粹的文化使者角色。可以说，“汤姆逊是第一个最广泛拍摄和传播中国的西方摄影家，是第一个对中国早期摄影术进行珍贵记录的摄影家，是第一个在拍摄中国人时孜孜追求摄影审美的艺术家和沟通大师，同时还是第一个广泛表现出对中国人民友好和同情的西方摄影家”。

汤姆逊去世后，他在中国拍摄的珍贵照片连同玻璃底版均被伦敦的维尔康姆图书馆收藏。虽然在图书馆的努力下，这批藏品得以系统地整理和编目，并接待了许多国家的研究学者，但对于照片诞生地的普罗大众来说，他们一直以来仍旧是遥远和陌生的。欣喜的是，在一个多世纪后的今天，在多方的努力下，中华世纪坛世界艺术馆终于迎来了“晚清碎影——汤姆逊眼中的中国（1868—1872）”摄影展，这次展览首次把汤姆逊的照片从遥远的英国带回来，并大规模地介绍给中国最广泛的观众群体。

在介绍的同时，展览还突出强调了一个“回望”的主题，这也正是中华世纪坛世界艺术馆2009年的业务主题——“回望中国”。当然，这种回望还不仅仅是我们自身对历史过往的回望，因为这些照片出自一个西方人的眼光，所以实际上这是一种跨越时间和地域的多角度的回望。既有过去的外国人如何看待当时的中国，又有现代的中国人如何看待自己的过去，当然还有现代的中国人透过外国人的眼光如何看待自己的过去等等。今天，当年费尽心力去记录和被记录的人俱往矣，但庆幸影像尚存，通过展览，这些影像又回到了当年场景的发生地——北京、福州、广州和东莞等地，它们将以见证者的身份去史海钩沉，并促使当代人去抚今追昔。

／王立梅，中华世纪坛世界艺术馆馆长
2009年4月

Foreword 1

More than a century ago the West opened China's gates with military force. What met their eyes was not just the huge quantity of raw materials such as fertile land, labour resources and export sites, but also an amazing sight of culture and history built up through several thousands of years of Chinese civilisation. As Western commodities rushed into the old China there followed many individuals who wanted to investigate this mysterious land and culture. The Scottish photographer John Thomson stood out among these visitors.

Thomson is known as one of the pioneers of photo-journalism. This is not just due to his extensive travels in Asia, including China but his choice to reach destinations in the interior previously undiscovered by foreign eyes, and also because of the unique era in which he traveled, when Chinese people knew next to nothing about photography. His powers of communication enabled him to capture the local customs and feelings of each place he visited, as he photographed Chinese people of all classes, from the aristocracy to the common man. More importantly, when compared with other foreign photographers in China during that era, his work is unaffected by racial prejudice but reflects an objective and realistic perspective of what he saw. Moreover, after his return to Britain, Thomson did his utmost to introduce these images of China to the West, through many illustrated lectures and numerous publications, he became one of the rare impartial cultural envoys of the time. It can be said that, "Thomson was the first Western photographer to disseminate images about China on such a wide scale, the first photographer to make such an earnest record of China, the first artist and master of communication to pursue with such devotion the aesthetics of photography. He was also the first Western photographer to extensively express kindness and empathy towards the Chinese people."

After his death, Thomson's collection of glass negatives of China were purchased by the Wellcome Library in London. Although the collection was well looked after and cataloged under the efforts of the Library and received the attention of many international scholars and researchers, the works however remained distant and estranged from the people of the land where they were created. It is wonderful that, today, more than one hundred years later, thanks to efforts from all sides, the Beijing World Art Museum is at last welcoming this exhibition " China – Through the Lens of John Thomson 1868 –1872" to China. This is the first time that Thomson's photographs have traveled this distance from Britain, to be viewed by their widest audience, the Chinese people.

The Beijing World Art Museum's theme for 2009 is "China Retrospect". "China – Through the Lens of John Thomson 1868 – 1872" will be one of the most important exhibitions of this year, placing emphasis on the theme of "looking back". Of course, this type of recollection is not as simple as looking back at our history from our own perspective, because these photographs also express the perspective of a Westerner, so this exhibition represents a multiple view that transcends different time and place. It captures how Westerners would have seen China at that time, how contemporary China sees its own history, and of course how modern day Chinese people see their past through the eyes a foreigner.

The photographer and his subjects are long gone, but their influence lives on. Through this exhibition audiences can retread their steps and return to the land where these images were captured, places such as Beijing, Fuzhou, Guangzhou and Dongguan, viewers can witness the past and treasure their memories.

／ Wang Limei, Director, Beijing World Art Museum
April, 2009

福建博物院
2009年6月13日-8月16日

Fujian Museum
13 June-16 August 2009

序　二

1868-1872年间，中国风雨飘摇的满清王朝正处在孕育着巨变的前夜，如果没有那些来自世界各地的摄影师的纪录，我们将永远丧失那个时代的许多历史瞬间和社会风俗画卷。苏格兰摄影师约翰·汤姆逊是来华纪实摄影师的先驱，他用相机客观地、真实地、艺术性地记录下19世纪中后期的中国社会面貌。

1839年银版摄影术的发明，正式拉开了现代摄影的序幕，而在此之后不到30年，西方摄影技术就随着约翰·汤姆逊来到中国，这些新发明的胶片记录下了封建社会后期那个在阵痛下裂变的中国。这些照片涉猎极广，涵盖了风光、人物、建筑、家庭、市井各个角度，让人们从不同的侧面了解到一百多年前的中国历史和文化。

本次展览的150幅照片，是汤姆逊作品在中国的首次大规模巡展，有许多都未曾与国人见面。这些珍贵照片具有双重的史料价值，不仅是那个时代中国人文景观的见证，同时也是展示早期摄影技术水平的重要资料。

同时，我们也希望通过此次展览，进一步增进中英两国人民之间的友谊和文化交流。

最后预祝展览圆满成功。

／杨琮，福建博物院院长
2009年4月

Foreword 2

During the period from 1868 to 1872, China stood precariously at the eve of a new era. The Qing Dynasty was enveloped by the forces of change. If not for those foreign photographers, record of many important historical moments and scenes of daily lives and customs of society would be lost forever. Scottish photographer John Thomson was a pioneer of photo-journalism, his objective, realistic and artistic perspective created a unique record of the face of Chinese society at the end of the 19th Century.

The invention of daguerreotype in 1839 launched the modern age of photography, and less than 30 years later Thomson brought this Western photographic technology with him to China. He used this newly invented wet collodian process to record the final years of feudal society as it broke up and the subsequent birth pains of a new age. These photographs touch on a broad range of subjects, covering many different themes such as landsccope, portraits, architecture, family, and urban life. They give people diverse perspectives through which to view and understand Chinese history and culture that was in existence over a century ago.

The 148 photographs to be shown are the first large scale shown of Thomson's work in China. Many of them have never been seen by the Chinese people. The historical value of these treasured images is twofold: they are not just a witness of views of Chinese culture and society at the time, but also an important resource of early photographic history and techniques.

We also hope this exhibition will advance friendly relations and cultural exchanges between the peoples of China and Britain.

I wish the exhibition great success.

／Yang Cong, Director, Fujian Museum
April, 2009

广州博物馆
2009年8月25日-9月25日

Guangzhou Museum
25 August-25 September 2009

序 三

从17世纪欧洲盛行“中国风”以来，中国文化一直吸引着无数欧美人士心向往之，并备受欧洲推崇，在欧洲近代社会发展过程中起到过较大影响。历史进入19世纪以后，西方文化逐渐占据强势地位，并深刻影响了中国近代历史进程。中国与欧洲这两种不同的文明由此在一种错综复杂的情形下进行交流与对话。而百年前的英国摄影师汤姆逊正是在这样的历史文化背景下，身扛笨重的摄影机，前来中国，并在中国大江南北一些重要的城市里，以他特有的审美视觉，有选择性地拍摄了不同社会阶层的风采，展示了东方人的审美情趣，留住了历史的瞬间，也为我们留下了一笔丰厚的文化遗产。今天，在中英两国文化人士的共同努力下，这批珍贵的历史照片沿着汤姆逊当年走过的足迹，分别到北京、福州、广州、东莞等城市巡展，特别是广州的展出地点定在广州博物馆馆址所在地镇海楼，则更是独具历史意义。因为这里不仅仅是广州的老城标，更是当年游历广州的欧洲画家笔下常见的风景。虽然汤姆逊的摄影作品中尚未见到有镇海楼的题材，但是却有镇海楼所在地越秀公园内的其他场景，所以我们可以肯定的是，汤姆逊到广州时一定曾远远望见过镇海楼。可以说，镇海楼是汤姆逊到广州进行拍摄时的历史见证者。

我们期待通过这次展览，让羊城人民更好地了解广州的过去，拓宽文化视野，增进与世界各国人民的友谊。

/程存洁，广州博物馆馆长
2009年4月

Foreword 3

Since the 17th Century when “Chinoiserie style” became fashionable in Europe, Chinese culture has attracted countless Europeans and Americans in search of something from the East. It has also had a relatively big influence on the development of Europe in modern times. After entering the 19th Century, Western culture gradually came to occupy a more forceful position, which deeply influenced the development of modern Chinese history. Because of this, exchange and communication between these two different cultures are enveloped by very complex attitudes and emotions.

It is against this historical and cultural background that the British photographer John Thomson arrived in China more than one hundred years ago. Coming to China, weighed down with cumbersome camera equipment, he traveled to important cities all over the country, to the north and south of the Yangtze River. With unique aesthetic vision he selectively photographed and captured the elegance of each different social class, showed the aesthetic flavour of the people of the Far East, leaving us with a record of an historical moment and a rich cultural treasure. Today, under the mutual efforts of Chinese and British cultural institutions and individuals, these treasured historical photographs have followed in the footsteps of Thomson over a century ago and are coming on an exhibition tour to cities such as Beijing, Fuzhou, Guangzhou and Dongguan. In Guangzhou they will be exhibited at the Guangzhou Museum's Zhenhai Tower with its unique historical significance. It is significant as a building because it not only represents the old city of Guangzhou, but because it was frequently painted by Western artists of the period. Although Thomson's works did not include scenes of the Zhenhai Tower itself, he did take an image of a memorial arch in the Yuexiu Park, therefore we can say for certain that on his travels to Guangzhou, the Tower would have attracted his gaze. It can be said that the Zhenhai Tower was a historical witness to the period of Thomson's travels to Guangzhou.

We eagerly await this exhibition and hope that it will help the people of Guangdong Province to better understand the past of Guangzhou, that it will broaden our cultural field of vision, and enhance friendly relations with people around the world.

/ Cheng Cunjie, Director, Guangzhou Museum
April, 2009

东莞展览馆
2009年11月3日-12月2日

Dongguan Exhibition Center
3 November-2 December 2009

序 四

一个多世纪以前，约翰·汤姆逊以一种对东方文化的好奇和对不同人种文化的偏好，以人类学、社会学的眼光，以摄影艺术家的敏锐为我们记录了大量珍贵的中国影像。“晚清碎影——汤姆逊眼中的中国（1868—1872）”摄影展使我们有幸欣赏到这些影像。

纵观汤姆逊拍摄的照片，他不仅拍摄了许多达官贵人与宫廷生活，而且还将摄影镜头对准了中国山水与普通百姓，拍摄了大量风土人情和普通人的生活，成为当时中国社会生活最真实的写照，对我们从一个侧面了解100多年前的中国历史和文化具有重要的价值。

汤姆逊拍摄的中国影像在19世纪的传播，大大促进了当时西方对中国的了解。时隔一个多世纪后，当他的作品返回中国之际，这些影像再次为我们架起了中西文化交流的桥梁，也让我们感受到了约翰·汤姆逊对中西文化交流的贡献。

东莞展览馆作为一座综合性的城市展览场馆，在着力宣传推介东莞的同时，亦致力于引进高品位的文化艺术展览，促进城市间的文化交流。作为“晚清碎影——汤姆逊眼中的中国（1868—1872）”的展出场馆之一，我们希望通过此次展览的举办，加强东莞市民对近代中国尤其是近代广东历史人文的认识与了解，感受近代来华的外国人眼中的中国风土人情，进一步增进中英两国间的文化交流。

感谢英国维尔康姆图书馆、中华世纪坛世界艺术馆为此次展览的举办所付出的努力！祝展出圆满成功！

/ 钟长永，东莞展览馆馆长
2009年4月

Foreword 4

More than one century ago, John Thomson traveled to China, filled with a curiosity about the Far East and a fondness for people of different cultures. From an anthropological and sociological perspective and with the keen aesthetics of a photographic artist he recorded a portrait of China that has become a great treasure. Through the exhibition " China – Through the Lens of John Thomson 1868 – 1872 we are very fortunate to be able to admire the images that he captured.

To look at Thomson's photographs in overall, we can see that he not only photographed the lives of the ruling classes and aristocracy, but also captured images of nature and of the common man. He photographed many images of the daily lives of common people, capturing their local customs and practices. His works are the most realistic portrayal of Chinese society of that period, and are most valued as a tool for us to understand Chinese history and culture from one hundred years ago.

The dissemination of Thomson's photographic portrait of China in the 19th Century greatly enhanced the West's understanding of China. Over a hundred years later, as these works return to China, once again we elevate the bridge of cultural exchange between the East and the West, and recognise Thomson's contribution towards this exchange.

The Dongguan Exhibition Centre is a comprehensive exhibition venue. As well as putting efforts into increasing knowledge and understanding of Dongguan, it is also dedicated to introducing quality international cultural and art exhibitions in order to advance cultural exchange between cities.

As one of the exhibition venues of "China – Through the Lens of John Thomson 1868 – 1872" we hope that through this exhibition we will strengthen Dongguan residents' understanding and knowledge of modern Chinese history, in particular modern history and culture of Guangdong Province. We hope that it will enable us to view foreign perspectives of 19th century Chinese and will also help to enhance cultural exchanges between China and Britain.

We would like to thank the Wellcome Library in Britain and the Beijing World Art Museum for all of their efforts in organising this exhibition. We wish it great success!

/ Zhong Changyong, Director, Dongguan Exhibition Centre
April, 2009

图1　Fig.1

人类的汤姆逊

/ 仝冰雪

如果当年伟大的马可·波罗能用几张照片来说明他漫游古老中国的经历，那么他的美丽传说会更加动人。

——约翰·汤姆逊

摄影术在1839年正式宣布发明后，伴随着第一次鸦片战争的炮火，也被西方人带入中国。在最早来中国摄影的几个西方人中，汤姆逊并未在其中之列：

第一个来中国摄影的外国人——法国人于勒·埃及尔
Jules Alphonse Eugène Itier，1802-1877，1844年来华；

第一个来中国的商业摄影师——瑞士人皮埃尔·罗西耶
Pierre Joseph Rossier，约1829-1898，1858年来华；

第一个大清都城的摄影师——意大利人菲利斯·比托
Felix Beato，约1825-1907，1860年来京；

但在中国的摄影史上，汤姆逊是第一个最广泛拍摄和传播中国的西方摄影家，是第一个对中国早期摄影术进行珍贵记录的摄影家，是第一个在拍摄中国人时孜孜追求摄影审美的艺术家和沟通大师，同时还是第一个广泛表现出对中国人民友好和同情的西方摄影家。

一、第一个最广泛拍摄和传播中国的西方摄影家

当研究上面提到的三位最早到中国的摄影师的照片时，我们会发现，于勒·埃及尔的银版摄影主要是在澳门和广州地区，拍摄数量极少；皮埃尔·罗西耶的立体照片拍摄只覆盖了香港和广东，而菲利斯·比托的湿版摄影也局限在香港、广州、天津、北京等几个城市。相比之下，约翰·汤姆逊的摄影作品则是第一次涵盖了中国的台湾、福建和长江流域的许多地区，他也成为西方第一个最广泛拍摄中国的摄影家。

回顾当时的摄影技术和中国人对摄影的认知，也许可以看出一个外国摄影师深入中国拍摄的难度。

John Thomson: A Humanist View of the World

/ Tong Bingxue

'Had the great Venetian traveler, Marco Polo, been able to confirm by a series of photographs his story of the wonders of Cathay, his fair fame would have escaped the discredit cast upon it for centuries, and indeed until comparatively recent investigation confirmed his story.'

– John Thomson

After its invention in 1839, photography was introduced into China by Europeans. John Thomson however, was not among the first photographers who visited China.

The French customs inspector and amateur daguerreotypist Jules Alphonse Eugène Itier (1802-1877) was the first person to bring photography into China (1844);

the Swiss pioneer photographer Pierre Joseph Rossier (c.1829 - c.1898) remained in China for several years from 1858, produced some of the first commercial photographs of China;

and the Venetian photographer Felice Beato (c.1825 - c.1907) arrived in imperial capital Beijing in 1860, took some of the first photographs of the Summer Palace.

In the history of photography in China, however, John Thomson was the first western photographer to have traveled and photographed so extensively and to have take up an active role informing the western audience about China the country. In his books on China, Thomson showed his genuine interest in the development of photography in China, while his photographs of the country and its people demonstrated he was not only an effective communicator and an excellent artist but also a human being with a profound love for China and deep feelings for its people.

1. Thomson´s work and legacy

Looking at photographs of China by Jules Alphonse Eugène Itier, Pierre Joseph Rossier and Felice Beato, we see that Itier mainly documented the conclusion of the Treaty of Whampoa and took a small number of daguerreotypes of Chinese people and scenery in Macau and the Guandong region. Rossier's stereographs covered mainly Hong Kong and Guangdong, while Beato's images were mainly about Taku forts in Tianjin, the Summer Palace in Beijing, and of Hong Kong and Guangdong. In comparison, Thomson was the first western photographer to travel and photograph so extensively across China from Formosa to Fujian and up the Yangtze River.

图2 Fig.2

图3 Fig.3

在1880年之前，摄影师采用的普遍是流行的湿版摄影法，摄影师不仅需要随身携带笨重的玻璃底板，还必须在拍摄现场涂布玻璃底板，现场显影和定影，因此需要随身携带移动暗房（一般是帐篷），各种药液甚至干净的清水。我们看看汤姆逊在中国的拍摄路线：广州、澳门、汕头、潮州、厦门、闽江、马尾、福州、台湾、香港、上海、胶州湾、天津、北京、上海、汉口、宜昌、九江、南京、上海、宁波等，近8000公里的行程。汤姆逊每次拍摄都需要雇佣多名"苦役"来背负笨重的照相器材，还要应对气候带来的困难：1871年冬天在胶州拍摄时，他刚把感光剂涂在玻璃上，玻璃就被冻住了，他只能找到炭火来融化。（图1）

汤姆逊作为商业摄影师，在深入内地的拍摄过程中，是没有外国部队的保护的。此外，汤姆逊不只是和中国的上流社会打交道，他更多地拍摄的是普通的中国人，这就要克服内地居民对摄影的恐惧。当时很多中国人认为照相机会把人的"灵魂"带走，摄影者甚至被认为是死亡的预言者，尤其当面对的是一个来自异国的白种人时，人们更为恐惧。汤姆逊亲眼看见有些中国人跪下哀求他不要把他们的影像乃至生命抓走。还有一次，他在广州拍摄古塔时，被人抓住推到江水里，幸亏被两个好心的中国姑娘搭救才得以逃脱。（图2）

今天，重新审视这一幅幅老照片，我们应当真诚地感谢汤姆逊，他的中国行程没有教会任务，没有外交使命，没有军事目的，也没有商业驱动，他完全以一种对中国的热爱，对东方文化的好奇和对不同人种文化的偏好，以人类学、社会学的眼光，以摄影艺术家的敏锐为我们记录了大量珍贵的中国影像。

汤姆逊当年对其所拍摄中国影像的有效传播，不仅使他本人获得了巨大的声誉，同时也极大促进了当时西方人对中国的了解。

早期来华摄影师一般都是通过销售原版照片册的方式来传播自己作品的，比如菲利斯·比托，而皮埃尔·罗西耶则通过售卖立体照片的方式来展示自己的中国影像。这样的方式不但局限性大，而且受众面很窄，此外还因所配照片文字太少而不易被人深入理解。而汤姆逊则采用出版有关中国的照片画册系列来展示自己的摄影成果，尤其是1873到1874年推出的《中国和中国人画报》（Illustrations of China and its People），采用凹版印刷的方式，展示了200幅他拍摄的中国照片精品，每幅照片都有记录式的文字说明，开创了利用摄影制版的印刷方式向西方大规模介绍报道中国和中国人民的先例，在欧洲引起了巨大反响，也成为世界摄影传播史上的一段佳话。

二、第一个对中国早期摄影术进行珍贵记录的摄影家

早期的摄影师在中国被认为是匠人，在正史中鲜有记载；并且因为早期照相机的昂贵，很少有照相楼同时拥有两部相机，因此，单独记载早期中国摄影师和照相楼的文字和图像资料十分少见。而约翰·汤姆逊关于香港和北京两地摄影实践的记录为我们研究中国早期摄影史提供了十分宝贵的资料。（图3）

在1872年11月29号和1872年12月13日出版的《英国摄影期刊》上，汤姆逊的两篇文章系统描述了在香港的中国摄影师的活动。他介绍说，在香港的皇后大道上，有20家中国人开的照相楼。其中，有个

It is not difficult to imagine how arduous it must have been for a western photographer to work in China at that time, carrying a large amount of cumbersome equipment while facing the suspicious eyes of the Chinese.

Until 1880, the wet-collodian process was the most advanced and popular photographic technique. For the coating and sensitizing of the plates and the developing and fixing of the image, a complete chest of chemicals was needed. Processing had to be carried out immediately before and after exposure of the plate in dark room conditions. A portable light-proof tent big enough to house the entire array of instruments – dishes, glass measures, funnels, scales, weights, etc., as well as the photographer himself, was essential, as was a bucket and supply of fresh water. With these equipment and supplies, and 'with the aid of eight to ten bearers' , Thomson sought to penetrate a largely unknown and unapproachable China, covering 8000 kilometres. Sometimes he experienced the extremes of temperature and on one occasion in winter 1871 while processing a picture of Chefoo, he poured some water over the glass negative and immediately the liquid froze on its surface. He had to thaw the negative over a charcoal fire and wash it clean with water.(Fig.1)

As an independent commercial photographer, Thomson was not accompanied by any foreign troops while traveling across inland China. In order to take photographs of ordinary Chinese, he often had to overcome people's fear of the camera. At the time it was a widespread belief that in taking a photograph a portion of the vital essence is extracted from the body of the sitter and imminent death is rendered an absolute certainty. Therefore a photographer was frequently looked upon as a forerunner of death, especially if he was a white foreigner. There were occasions when Thomson witnessed some Chinese so stricken with superstitious dread that they fell down on bended knees and beseeched him not to take their likeness with the fatal lens of his camera. On another occasion, when he was attempting to take a photograph of a tower not far from Guangdong, Thomson was assailed on the river bank by a mob of ruffians, who drove him into the river. Luckily he was taken into a boat by a couple of good-natured women. (Fig.2)

Today as we re-examine Thomson's photographs of China and its people, we feel we owe him a debt of gratitude. Out of pure curiosity for Eastern culture and love for China, he captured the day-to-day lives of the people and a great number of remarkable images of a fragile nation in the process of change. They were the first photographic social documentation of China to be published. These images not only showed Thomson's remarkable talent as a photographer, they also contributed a great deal to the 19th century western view of China and its people.

Whilst Pierre Joseph Rossier and Felice Beato's photographs were sold individually and so had a very limited audience, Thomson was the first to publish his works in book format. *Illustrations of China and its People* first appeared in 1873, with 200 engravings made from Thomson's photographs. These photographs were printed by the newly invented collotype process and the images were accompanied by Thomson's own text in which he frequently displayed remarkable knowledge, insight and wit. It caused a stir in Europe.

2. History of photography in 19th century China

In Chinese historical documents photographers were considered artisans. At that time, cameras were very

叫阿芳（Afong Photographer）的摄影师"有良好的艺术修养，凭他的才能，甚至在伦敦也能立足"。他随后详细描写了一个叫"A-Hung"的中国人经营的照相楼，向我们全面展示了一个清代中国照相馆的生动写照：

进入摆满广告肖像照片的门口，登上窄窄的楼梯来到二楼的接待室，正在光着膀子的A-Hung赶紧穿上衬衫，用洋泾浜英语和汤姆逊打着招呼。随后A-Hung向汤姆逊介绍了中国人的摄影趣味，他说西方人总喜欢在摄影时脱离直线和垂线，而中国人喜欢直视镜头，脸部没有阴影，这样他们的朋友在远处观看照片时就能看到他们的双眼和双耳，也才能体现出一个人的全部容貌。但是受西方摄影教育的汤姆逊并不赞同这个观点，认为这样的构图太平淡了，还和A-Hung争论起来。最后，汤姆逊开玩笑地说：如果为了展示一个人的全貌，你为什么不把人的后背和辫子也照一张，贴在正面照片的后面呢？A-Hung丝毫没有示弱，风趣地说：好建议，我考虑考虑!

随后，他跟随A-Hung来到了另外一个小屋里。墙上挂满了肖像照片，也有画在帆布上的油画肖像。当时很多照相楼同时经营画像业务，这些肖像大部分是外国人，也有很多舰船画像。四五个光着脊背，下穿绸裤的中国画家口含烟斗，一边对着照片画像，一边聊天，其中一人还在阳光中哼着小曲，一派其乐融融的景象。

A-Hung为本地几个穿着节日盛装的男女拍摄了照片，他们都是一个姿势，旁边是一方几，几上的花瓶里插着一束假花，背景布上装饰着两个窗帘。A-Hung给汤姆逊精心挑选的几张照片上的人脸都看起来很白，很平淡，汤姆逊打趣地说：你拍摄的人好像刚刚在石灰水里泡过了。A-Hung得意地说：是的，我觉得你应当喜欢他们，他们很精美，我是通过给拍摄者脸上擦粉才得到这样的效果的。照相的玻璃屋里很热，拍摄者一坐下就会出汗，这样擦的粉就会很好地粘在脸上。不但本地人，连马来人和黑人到这里照相都是采用这种方法，效果很好，成本低得更是不值一提。

A-Hung为本地人拍照的费用是12张（名片照片）收费8先令，同时，他也复制一些欧洲人拍摄的照片在自己的店里销售，这样的照片是12张收费2先令。

最后，汤姆逊来到了照相的玻璃屋子里，阳光从上面照下来，令人眩目，他们坐在座位上，颈部和四肢被照相专用的铁支架固定住，然后相机被拉过来瞄准他们，长时间的曝光好像经历了一个世纪，最后当他们听到敲击帽子的声音时，发现终于拍摄完成了。A-Hung消失在旁边的暗房里，从一个小窗户里，汤姆逊听到他在数底板：一号！

汤姆逊从照相房间出来后，再次环顾外屋的画师，在角落里看到一个看起来比实际年龄长20岁的老者。他是一个在象牙上作画的缩微画师，但他每天也就工作不超过两三个小时，其余时间在吸食鸦片和午休。对比周围索然无味的工作环境，很难想象他们能够画出如此精致和美丽的缩微肖像。他们的画像主要是根据顾客的照片而作，每当顾客需要一幅缩微画像时，他们就会在顾客的照片上罩住一个带方格的玻璃，把照片分割成不同的方块，用铅笔在象牙上画草图，然后再根据照片内容填充。同样的方法也用在画大幅的油画肖像上，但这样的油画画得不是特别精确——因为一般是几个画师合作完成一幅画，技艺高超的画师画头部，次等的画师画手部，学徒画服饰和珠宝。绘制一幅18×12英寸的画像大约需要30先令，对经常光顾港口的外国海员来说，为他们的朋友或先人画像带回国内，是一份不错的纪念品。

从汤姆逊的记载中可以看出，脱胎于早期画楼的照相馆，还保留了画楼的很多业务，这是和早期摄

expensive and a studio rarely had more than one camera. Therefore, there were very few records of early Chinese photographers nor their photographs. Thomson's work provides us with invaluable visual and historical documentation in understanding 19th century China and its early history of photography. (Fig.3)

In 1872 Thomson contributed two articles to the *British Journal of Photography*. He recounts the activities of early Chinese photographers and portrait artists working in Hong Kong. According to him, on Queen's Road Central, there were about 20 photographic and artist studios and amongst them was Afong Studio owned by the Chinese photographer Lai Afong. He 'was a plump and good natured son of Han', Thomson recalls and 'a man of exquisite taste.'

According to Thomson there were a number of painters established in Hong-Kong but they all did the same class of work and have about the same tariff of prices, regulated according to the dimensions of the canvas. The occupation of these painters consisted mainly in making enlarged copies of photographs. In one such artist studio Thomson noted that its walls were adorned with paintings in oil and some of the specimens of photographic art displayed in doorways were fairly good. 'The work in this painting-shop, like many things Chinese, is so divided as to afford the maximum of profit for the minimum of labour. Thus one artist sketches, another paints the face, a third does the hands, and a fourth fills in the costume and accessories. A canvas portrait is placed on the artist's easel, and is covered with a piece of glass bearing the lines and squares which solve the problem of proportion in the large work.' In one corner of the studio, Thomson noticed that one artist had just roused himself from a long sleep and his clothes were redolent of the fumes of opium: 'he peers through his large spectacles into the subject's black eyes, and measures out her fair proportions as he transfers them to the canvas; then she is passed from hand to hand, until at last every detail has been produced with pre-Raphaelite exactitude, and a glow of colour added to the whole, far surpassing nature.'

Here Thomson was told that 'a Chinaman would not suffer himself to be posed so as to produce a profile or three-quarter face, his reason being that the portrait must show him to possess two eyes and two ears and that his round face is perfect as a full moon. The same observance of symmetry is carried out in the entire pose of the figure; the face too must be as nearly as possible devoid of shadow, or if there be any shadow at all, it must be equal on both sides; this love of symmetry is also observed in carrying two watches in place of one in pockets placed one each side of the coat. Shadow, the Chinese say, should not exist; it is an accident of nature, and therefore should not be portrayed, as it does not represent any feature of the face'; 'and yet', commented Thomson, 'they all of them carry fans in order to secure that very shade so essential to existence in the South of China!'

These early accounts of Chinese photographic studios have left us with an invaluable historical record of early Chinese photography.

In comparison to Hong Kong, in the imperial capital Beijing, the first photographic studio only emerged in 1879. Thomson's 1898 book *Through China with a Camera* provided us with a vivid account of early photographic activities in the city. As Thomson shows, already in 1871, there were at least two people in Beijing devoted to photography. One such person was a Mr Wang, a man with some imperial connections who accompanied Thomson when he photographed the ruins of the Summer Palace. The other, was a businessman, Mr.Yang, 'a fine sample of the modern Chinese savant — fat, good-natured and contented, but much inclined to take short cuts to scientific knowledge,

图4 Fig.4

图5 Fig.5

图6 Fig.6

影技术的发展必然相关的。因为那时没有放大技术，没有彩色技术，而国外市场对大的彩色肖像仍然有巨大的需求，加上中国便宜的劳动力资源，因此，画像和摄影并存，成为早期中国照相馆的一大特色。汤姆逊的那张正在画像的画师的照片也为我们考证早期中国摄影的发展提供了影像实证。

和香港早期繁荣的商业摄影相比，当时的大清都城北京却是另外一番景象。北京最早一家中国人从事的商业摄影是成立于1879年的丰泰照相馆，由辽宁法库人任庆泰创办。在这之前，虽然1860年英国战地摄影师费里斯·比托拍摄了大量北京的照片并得到广泛传播，但在1860到1879近二十年间，中国人的摄影实践鲜有记录，而约翰·汤姆逊在1899年出版的《镜头前的中国》（Through China with a Camera）一书中的有关描述为我们研究北京早期摄影史提供了宝贵的史料。（图4）

根据约翰逊的记载，到1871年，至少有两位北京人在进行摄影实践活动。一位是王先生，陪同约翰逊去了西郊的皇家园林——颐和园拍摄，王先生是当时北京工部的一位高官；另外一位叫杨方（音译），他是一所当铺的老板，早年在上海接受的教育，也学会了很多时髦的知识和西化的生活方式，很愿意和北京的外国人交朋友。杨方邀请汤姆逊到家里做客，汤姆逊发现杨先生在家里建立了一个摄影室，自己动手配制药液，为家人拍摄了大量肖像照片，挂在自家的墙壁上。杨方还和汤姆逊交流了摄影的心得。虽然在汤姆逊的眼里，王先生和杨方还属于业余摄影师，但说明在当时的大清禁地，在皇室还没有接受摄影术的情况下，摄影术已经在上流社会和民间都生根发芽了。

三、第一个在拍摄中国人时孜孜追求摄影审美的艺术家和沟通大师

汤姆逊在香港曾广泛地和中国摄影师交往，比如上面我们曾提到了他和A-Hung有关人像摄影角度和光线的辩论。他在相关书籍中曾提到：中国人喜欢全身照，喜欢左右对称，不喜欢脸上有阴影。受到西方正统教育的汤姆逊，对中国人的摄影审美虽然能够理解，但他在摄影创作中，并没有像很多当地的外国摄影师那样单纯地迎合本地市场需求，仍然坚持以自己的艺术理念拍摄了大量中国人的肖像，为我们从另外一个视角保存了一份早期的历史遗存。（图5）

比如在新加坡和香港，他在对中国人的商业肖像拍摄中拍摄了大量中国人的侧面肖像，半身照片或头部特写。作为一个商业摄影师，这样做是要冒风险的，因为很多中国客户并不喜欢这样的作品。当然在旅行拍摄中，汤姆逊也保持了他一贯的艺术创作风格，有意识地摄制了大量的特写肖像，我们可以在这次展览中充分欣赏到。

另外，汤姆逊有意识地发现平凡生活之美。比如他拍摄了大量中国妇女发式的特写照片，拍摄了大量妇女头饰的影像，从沿海的香港、厦门、福州到内地北京，从客家农妇到满清格格，这些珍贵的照片对我们研究清末女子头饰和服饰演变提供了珍贵的参考。（图6）

当今天我们仔细审视汤姆逊拍摄的影像时，还是会被汤姆逊杰出的沟通才能所折服。

我们知道，汤姆逊所使用的照相机，根据光线强度不同，曝光时间不等，但都是几秒甚至十几秒钟。但我发现，汤姆逊有意识地脱离了早期传统拍摄静态人物的方式，拍摄了大量动态的肖像和群体照片。比如：正在喊号的更夫，正在给小姐梳头的丫鬟，正在磨刀的匠人等，这些照片不是我们今天抓拍

and to esteem his own incomplete and haphazard achievements the results of marvelously perfect intelligence.' Mr. Yang was an amateur photographer who had a private laboratory in his huge house and its walls were 'garnished with enlarged photographs of Yang's family and friends.' (Fig.4)

3. Thomson – the artist and the man

Throughout his journey in China, Thomson never ceased to communicate with local people and in Hong Kong he often discussed photography techniques with local artists. Unlike many of his contemporaries, Thomson did not pursue purely commercial success. In Singapore and Hong Kong, he took a number of half portraits and head shots. To a commercial photographer, this carried a certain risk because the majority of Chinese customers preferred full body portraiture. In fact, as this exhibition shows, portraiture was an integral part of Thomson's work: from formal portraits of rulers and gentry to images of Chinese women with different types of coiffeur. Even when he was travelling, Thomson did not stop making portraits. These provide us with an important historical reference for the study of costumes and hairstyles of the late Qing period. (Fig.5, 6)

To take such images required a high level of communication between the photographer and his subjects, especially when trying to photograph among 'a people hostile to foreigners'. Often, Thomson would suggest that subjects change their position or gesture so they would feel more at ease. Images of couples facing each other were highly unusual in imperial China, but Thomson was successful in taking a number of those. At times, there was a price to pay. For instance, Thomson had to bribe a woman handsomely in order to photograph her golden lilies, a euphemism for bound feet. Money was at times a way to communicate with the locals, as he wrote once 'we offered one or two small silver coins to the children of the house but the old gentleman would not permit them to be accepted until it had been carefully explained to him that they were simply gifts to be worn as charms and not intended as a recompense for his hospitality.' (Fig.7)

4. Thomson and China

Unlike many of his contemporaries, Thomson was not, as might be expected, attached to any government survey neither was he on an official mission. He went to China out of curiosity. While there, he gradually developed a profound love for the country and a deep sympathy for its people. There were no distorted images of China and in Thomson's photos we see human individuals full of peculiarities - we see them smiling and relaxing.

Although Thomson was very critical of the corrupt Qing government he said reform should 'begin with the government itself, however with the people of China, Thomson experienced 'many instances of a simple genuine hospitality' 'all over the land; and I feel assured that any foreigner knowing enough of the language to make his immediate wants understood, and endowed with a reasonable even temper, would encounter little opposition in traveling over the greater part of China.' This positive feeling Thomson held towards Chinese people can be seen through his photographs.

图7 Fig.7

图8 Fig.8

图9 Fig.9

那么简单，而需要耐心地和被摄者沟通，甚至让他们保持某个姿态。虽然汤姆逊有中国助手和翻译，但在当时摄影术并不太受欢迎的中国，尤其是在内陆地区，需要摄影师在一个尽可能短的时间内说服被拍摄者配合，比如如何保持姿势，尤其是保持一个真实、放松的姿势，这里面需要极大的和真诚的沟通能力。（图7）

在汤姆逊拍摄的中国人肖像中，有不少夫妻对视、母子相望、主仆眼神交流的照片，这是不符合当时中国传统习俗的，有人说，这都是当时外国人给拍摄者银两才达到的效果。确实，在当时有很多外国摄影师为了让中国人配合拍照都给一些所谓的"报酬"，但我认为，取得这样的效果更多是来自汤姆逊真诚的沟通和杰出的导演才能。他曾在游记中写道："我主动给了住所里的小孩几个银币，但是一位老绅士不许他们接受。经过我再三解释说，这是有着吉祥象征的礼物，并非有意作为对其殷勤款待的报酬，他们才勉强收下"。可见在和中国人打交道的过程中，汤姆逊在尊重中国风俗的基础上表现出了充分的灵活性，这样也使他能够拍摄出一般西方摄影师难以达到的效果。

四、第一个对中国人民广泛友好和同情的西方摄影家

翻看西方摄影师早期在中国拍摄的照片，大部分人是抱有一种猎奇的心态，对中国人充满了敌意和曲解。因此，小脚女人、乞丐等社会阴暗面成为摄影师拍摄的主题，拍摄的人物大都神情木讷、呆板。而当我审视汤姆逊拍摄的中国照片时，我看到更多的是中国人的笑脸，看到了更多放松的中国人。

当汤姆逊来到中国时，虽然他也深感清政府的腐败，觉得"改革应当是政府本身的改革"（《镜头前的旧中国》，第5页，中国摄影出版社，2001年7月），而对中国人民，汤姆逊用切身体会说道："我在中国的感受是：中国人相当诚恳、好客。我相信任何一个能用语言表达自己思想并能使对方理解的外国人，在中国大部分的旅途中不会遇到什么敌意的对待"。可以看出，汤姆逊对中国人民的态度是友善的，对中国人民是抱有同情心的，这种思想感情也表现在他的许多作品中。（图8，图9）

纵观汤姆逊拍摄的中国照片，虽然他也拍摄了达官贵人、风景名胜，但他拍摄更多的是大量普通人的生活和街头小景。在这些照片中，我们看到了很多悠闲的市民小姐，也看到了街边正在享受午餐的"苦力"，还有正沉浸在欣赏"西洋景"的孩子们。可以说，在汤姆逊的镜头下，我们发现了许许多多大清帝国臣民纯朴、美好的侧面，这样的影像不论在早期外国摄影师还是中国照相馆的拍摄中都是很少见的。在一张旗人女子梳头的照片中，端坐的小姐自然，放松，面带微笑，旁边站立的丫环面容敦厚，神情专注，而一侧的孩童天真无邪。这张照片即使放在今天来看，依然有着强烈的艺术感染力。在北京拍摄满族新娘的照片时，汤姆逊也了解到了这个新人未来在传统家庭中的低贱地位。凝视照片，当我们被新娘精美的头饰和华丽的盛装所吸引后，却更被新娘那忧郁的眼神和无奈的神情所打动，这些也正是作为摄影师的汤姆逊其同情心的真实写照。

A quick look through Thomson's photographs, show that his works were not merely portraits of rulers and landed gentry and panoramic landscapes. In China he photographed many anonymous individuals in street scenes and at their homes. He was very sensitive to human beings, and this was projected through his images: from coolies enjoying their roadside lunch, to children watching a peep show, a Manchu woman dressing her hair and a bride in her beautiful wedding costume, though with a hint of sadness in her eyes.

For Thomson, his China journey was remarkable and provided him with a wealth of experience as a photographer. His photographs contributed greatly to 19th century Europe's understanding of Asia and filled the visual gap between East and West. He became known as 'China' Thomson. Perhaps even more importantly, his images of China and its people, as well as his later images of London street scenes, present to us a humanist view of the world. (Fig.8，9)

In his *Through China with a Camera*, Thomson wrote: 'I will conclude this introductory sketch by expressing the hope that China may awake from her lethargy before it is too late'. More than a century later, these images are finally brought back to China. Let's hope his wish will become true.

汤姆逊曾说，他在中国的经历是"愉快"的。在他的游记中，我们也可以充分感受到汤姆逊积极的生活态度和一种博爱的心态。在西方，汤姆逊曾经因为他对中国地形学和民族志学的记录而赢得了"中国的汤姆逊"的绰号，今天，回望汤姆逊镜头下美丽的中国，我们也应该亲切地称他为"中国的汤姆逊"。正像汤姆逊回到伦敦后因关注当地百姓疾苦而赢得"街头摄影家"的赞誉一样，他的这种博爱不是一种狭隘的民族偏好，是他对人类普遍的同情心使然，因此，我们更应当称呼他为"人类的汤姆逊"！

1898年，汤姆逊在他最后一部关于中国的出版物《镜头前的中国》第一章结束时曾说："我希望中国能够尽快从他毫无生气的现状中觉醒"。一个多世纪过去了，在他的作品再次返回家乡之际，他善良的愿望也正在这里变成现实！

参考书目或文献：

1. 杨博仁、陈宪平译：《镜头前的旧中国——约翰·汤姆森游记》，中国摄影出版社，2001年7月第一版第一次印刷。
2. 王大正："中国电影的创始人——任庆泰"，《当代电影》，2005年第六期。
3. Nick Pearce, Photographs of Peking, China 1861-1908, Ceredigion: The Edwin Mellen Press UK, 2005
4. John Thomson, China and its people in early photographs, New York: Dover Pubication, Inc., 1982
5. John Thomson, China and its People, a catalogue by The British Council, 1991
6. Wue, Roberta; Lai, Edwin K.; Waley-Cohen, Joanna, Picturing Hong Kong, photographs1955-1910, New York & Hong Kong: Asia Society in association with South China Printing Company, 1998
7. Regine Thiriez, Barbarian Lens, Western Photographers of the Qianlong Emperor's European Palaces, Gordon and Breach Publisher, 1998
8. John Thomson, Illustrations of China and its People, London: Sampson Low and Searle, 1873-1874
9. John Thomson, Through China with a Camera, Westminster: A Constable & Co., 1898

A Selected Bibliography:

1. Nick Pearce, Photographs of Peking, China 1861-1908, Ceredigion: The Edwin Mellen Press UK, 2005
2. John Thomson, China and its people in early photographs, New York: Dover Pubication, Inc., 1982
3. John Thomson, China and its People, a catalogue by The British Council, 1991
4. Wue, Roberta; Lai, Edwin K.; Waley-Cohen, Joanna, Picturing Hong Kong, photographs1955-1910, New York & Hong Kong: Asia Society in association with South China Printing Company, 1998
5. Regine Thiriez, Barbarian Lens, Western Photographers of the Qianlong Emperor's European Palaces, Gordon and Breach Publisher, 1998
6. John Thomson, Illustrations of China and its People, London: Sampson Low and Searle, 1873-1874
7. John Thomson, Through China with a Camera, Westminster: A Constable & Co., 1898
8. Wang Dazheng, 'Zhongguo dianying de chuangshiren – Ren Qingtai' (Ren Qingtai and Early Chinese Cinema), in Dangdai dianying, no. 6, 2005

约翰·汤姆逊：从伦敦到中国，从中国到伦敦

/威廉·舒巴赫，维尔康姆图书馆

让我们回到歇洛克·福尔摩斯时代的伦敦。浓雾中走来一位拄着手杖的老人，他从位于伦敦南部朴素的家中出发，沿着伦敦西区的时髦街道，穿过古典样式的豪华办公楼，去参观一个正在公开展示的新收藏：这些古物在威格莫尔街的一个展厅中展出，收藏者是一位富有的美国药剂师：亨利·S·维尔康姆。

来参观的老人是摄影师约翰·汤姆逊，那年是1920年，他已经83岁了。而在其青壮年时期，他曾是一个伟大的旅行家。从19世纪60年代开始，汤姆逊从故乡苏格兰出发，游历了远东很多地方。在岷江湍急的河流中，他险些遭遇翻船；在山东，当他试图拍摄一座横跨河上的古桥时，桥上的人们向他投掷石块，以至于他不得不用相机的三脚架来保护自己；在中国西部边远的山村，他是当地人见到的第一个欧洲人；他还曾与泰国国王孟库一世会谈，并穿过柬埔寨战争区到达了宏伟的吴哥城与吴哥窟遗址；在北京，他既拍摄到道光皇帝的六子——尊贵的恭亲王奕䜣，也把镜头对向在胡同中走街串巷吆喝着卖瓷器的小贩；他曾勇敢地深入充满沼气的塞浦路斯沼泽去拍摄当地人的起居，在伦敦，他也无时无刻不在关注那些生活在维多利亚女王足下的底层贫民，而同时，他也被邀请为女王留影。

回到英国后，汤姆逊出版了很多介绍其旅行的书，也拥有了大量的玻璃底版，这些底版是他为了印制出版物而于数十年前从中国和其他地方带回来的。

1920年，汤姆逊在维尔康姆的这个历史展上，一定是看到了走廊上挂着的那排已经归属于维尔康姆私人财产的照片：那可以说是一个小型展览，内容大部分是关于非洲的，但没有中国。所以，在1920年5月12日，汤姆逊写信给画廊的主管：

> 亲爱的先生，我不知道维尔康姆先生是否有意在博物馆中辟出一间屋子专门用作照片展示。如果有此打算，那么选取一些我在东方拍摄的照片将会是有价值的，因为每张照片都再现了我所到之处的某些独特的风土人情。每个系列都包括了如文物、艺术、建筑、工业和发展见证等主题，地区涵盖了暹罗、交趾支那、柬埔寨、中国和塞浦路斯。我可以提供每个主题的底版和文字注释。我敢肯定，这些系列会有助于提升博物馆本已相当精彩的藏品规模和趣味性。真心希望得到您的意见。
>
> 约翰·汤姆逊

John Thomson: London to China, China to London

/ William Schupbach, Wellcome Library

We are in the London of Sherlock Holmes. Through the fog walks an elderly man with a stick. He makes his way along the streets in the smart West End with its lavish new office buildings in the classical style. He is on a trip from his modest home in Streatham in south London to see a new collection that has gone on public display: the exhibition, in a showroom in Wigmore Street, of historical artefacts belonging to the wealthy American pharmaceutical manufacturer, Henry S. Wellcome.

The elderly man is the photographer John Thomson, and the date is 1920, when he is 83 years old. In his youth and middle age he had been a great traveller. He had set off from his native Scotland in the 1860s and had travelled widely in the Far East. On the River Min rapids he had been shipwrecked. In Shantou, as he tried to photograph an ancient bridge over the river, the people on the bridge pelted him so that he was forced to defend himself with the tripod of his camera. He had been the first European to be seen by the inhabitants of the villages he had passed through in Western China. He had conversed with King Mongkut I of Thailand, and had made his way through the Cambodian jungle to find the colossal ruins of Angkor Wat and Angkor Tom. In Beijing he had photographed the admired Yi Xin (Prince Gong), sixth son of Emperor Daoguang, and he had photographed the street traders shouting out their wares amidst the crowded hutongs. He had braved the malarial swamps of Cyprus to photograph the Cypriot families in their rustic houses, and in London he had captured for all time the sufferings of the poorest class under Queen Victoria--whose photograph he had also been invited to take.

After his return to Great Britain, he had published many books on his travels, and was in possession of a large number of the glass negatives, which, decades before, he had brought back from China and elsewhere for reproduction in his publications.

On his visit to the Wellcome historical exhibition in 1920, Thomson would have seen a corridor lined with photographs already in Wellcome's possession: it was a small display and had much about Africa but nothing about China. So, on 12 May 1920, Thomson wrote to the curator of the gallery:

> Dear Sir, I don't know if Mr Wellcome intends to have a room in the museum set apart for the exhibition of photographs. If he does, selections from the photographs taken by me during my eastern travels would prove useful, seeing that each photograph was taken to represent something peculiar to the lands and to the people I visited. Each series includes antiquities, arts, architecture, industries, and evidence of evolution. The regions include Siam, Cochin China, Cambodia, China and the islands of Formosa and Cyprus. I would supply the negatives and quotable notes to each subject. I am sure that such a series would add usefulness and interest to the wonderful collection of this museum. Kindly let me know your views on the subject. Yours sincerely, J. Thomson.

这封信可看做是拉开了我们当前此次摄影展的序幕。如果汤姆逊没有写这封信，展览的照片未必能留存至今。因为当时很少有机构会愿意负责如此多的工作：保存大量沉重的旧式玻璃底版，从负片洗印照片，编辑目录以及提供给全世界范围内的展览和研究。

汤姆逊希望维尔康姆能为他的摄影作品提供一间展室，这自然是一个合理的要求。因为维尔康姆自己也是个热心摄影的业余爱好者，他配制摄影用的化学试剂，出版摄影家年鉴，并建立起一个涵盖了很多大师作品的历史照片收藏库，其中包括：德西雷·沙尔奈拍摄的墨西哥风景，爱德华-德尼·鲍尔达拍摄的法国中世纪，爱德华·S·柯蒂斯拍摄的美洲土著人肖像，朱利亚·马格利特·卡梅伦拍摄的英国人肖像，塞缪尔·伯恩考察克什米尔的获奖作品。现在，汤姆逊的作品，与费利斯·比图和威廉·普赖尔·弗洛伊德这些均于19世纪曾拍摄过中国的摄影师的作品一道，也被纳入到此精美照片的宝库中。

但汤姆逊本人并没能等到将自己的摄影并入到维尔康姆的收藏就去世了，维尔康姆随后从汤姆逊的后人手上购买了他的作品。最终，三个金属边的大木箱子装着珍贵的底版被运到了维尔康姆的办公室，随后成为维尔康姆图书馆收藏的一部分，并保存至今。自1981年起，这批藏品被整理编目，并有许多中国、泰国、苏格兰、法国和美国的学者去研究。在研究过程中，人们找到许多在任何一本汤姆逊已经出版的书上都没有出现过的新照片，这些底版也成为它们所展现的那个场景的唯一见证物了。另外还有一些照片虽然发表过，但却被裁切过，以至于读者只能看到位于全画面中间的人物，而无法得知实际上在未剪裁的原图上显示出这个人是坐在皇宫花园或是户外的堤岸上。

除了照片本身所呈现的比例和内容，人们还可以更深入地研究和欣赏汤姆逊的艺术风格。因此，维尔康姆图书馆非常欣喜于这个即将开幕的展览，因为它将把汤姆逊最具人文性和启发性的照片介绍给新的观众们。

That letter was the beginning of the process that has led to the present exhibition. If Thomson had not written it, it is unlikely that the photographs in this exhibition would exist today: there were few institutions at the time that could have taken on the responsibility of preserving such a huge weight of old glass, making positive prints from the negatives, making a catalogue of them, and making them available worldwide for exhibition and research.

Thomson's hope that Wellcome would provide a home for his photographs was a reasonable one: Wellcome was himself an enthusiastic amateur photographer, he manufactured photographic chemicals, published a photographer's annual diary, and was building up a collection of historic photographs that would include works by many master photographers: views of Mexico by Désiré Charnay, records of mediaeval France by Édouard-Denis Baldus, portraits of native Americans by Edward S. Curtis and of English men and women by Julia Margaret Cameron, and prize-winning studies of Kashmir by Samuel Bourne. Within this treasure-house of fine photographs, Thomson, along with Felice Beato and William Pryor Floyd, would represent those who had photographed China in the nineteenth century.

Thomson died before the negotiations to add his photographs to the collection were concluded, and Wellcome subsequently bought them from Thomson's heirs. As a result, three wooden steel-lined crates containing the precious negatives were delivered to the Wellcome offices and subsequently became part of the Wellcome Library, where the crates and their original contents are preserved today. Since 1981 they have been catalogued and studied with the aid of many scholars from China, Thailand, Scotland, England, France and America. In the course of these studies, the collection was found to contain many photographs that Thomson had not been able to include in any of his publications: these negatives are the sole surviving witnesses of the scenes that they show. Others were published but in a cropped form, so that readers of Thomson's publications only saw the people in the centre of a composition, unaware that the uncropped original negative showed the people sitting in a palace garden or out on the Bund.

Given the size and range of Thomson's work, there is still much scope for further study and enjoyment of his art. The Wellcome Library is therefore delighted that the present exhibition will bring Thomson's most humane and evocative photographs to new audiences.

汤姆逊的中国照片和维尔康姆图书馆

/ 周迅

摄影师约翰·汤姆逊

约翰·汤姆逊（1837－1921）生于英国爱丁堡。在他出生两年之后，摄影术的始祖——银版照相法问世。同年，福克斯·塔尔博特发明了卡罗版摄影法（亦称碘化银法）。爱丁堡的两位著名摄影家奥克塔维厄·希尔和罗伯特·亚当斯运用这种新技术拍摄了近3000幅照片，题材涉及城市景观、自然风光和日常生活。这些作品无疑对汤姆逊产生了深刻的影响。

就在汤姆逊成为职业摄影家之前的短短二十年中，摄影术的发展堪称日新月异。而诞生于1850年的火胶棉湿版法则是一个重要的里程碑。它降低了曝光时间和摄影的成本，生成的影像也更加清晰锐利，因此迅速取代了银版照相法和卡罗版法。正如汤姆逊所说："火胶棉湿版法的底版影像细节纤毫毕现，过渡自然，冲印出的照片质量更是任何现有技术所无法超越的"。但是火胶棉湿版法本身有一个很大的缺点：因为曝光之前需要在玻璃板上涂布火胶棉乳液，所以摄影师不得不随身携带大量笨重的设备。

但是汤姆逊没有在困难面前退缩。作为一个维多利亚时代的人，他所接受的严格教育使他养成了不畏难苦、坚韧不拔的个性和强健的体魄。同时，作为维多利亚时代的人，他与许多同时代人一样为刚刚开拓的非洲和亚洲而感到激动；他们对探索异域他乡充满了热情。他深信摄影"不仅能给探险家带来更多的乐趣，也使他们的工作具有不朽的价值"。而"在这个知识和教育至上的时代，照相机应当成为教育这个时代的强有力的工具"。

1862年，汤姆逊启程前往新加坡，在当地开办了一家照相馆，成为一名专业人像摄影师。在此期间，他对当地的风土人情产生了浓厚的兴趣。随后，汤姆逊到马来西亚和苏门答腊拍摄了不少风光与人物照片。1866年，汤姆逊迁居曼谷，并首次前往柬埔寨和印度支那（越南）拍摄。这些柬埔寨与暹罗题材的摄影作品使他成为一名颇有声誉的旅游摄影师，他也因此被选为伦敦民族志学会和皇家地理学会的会员。

1868年，汤姆逊第二次来到亚洲，居住在繁华的英国殖民地香港。在这里，他学习了汉语和中国文化，并几次短暂前往广东。而汤姆逊最为重要的中国之旅始于1870年，为时两年。在这两年中，他从广东进入福建，然后游历了华东和华北，并到达了都城北京；此后他又南下长江流域，其行程长达8000多公里。他此行所拍摄的作品在影像质量、内容深刻性、题材广泛性和作品艺术性等方面都达到了新的高度。特别是他在北京拍摄那些以街头和社会为背景照片时所积累的摄影经验和技术为他五年后创作《伦

Thomson's China photographs and the Wellcome Library

/ Zhou Xun

Thomson the photographer

John Thomson (1837–1921) was born in Edinburgh two years before the invention of the daguerreotype was announced to the world in 1839. This discovery was the beginning of photography. That same year, Fox Talbot introduced the calotype process, and with this new medium David Octavius Hill and Robert Adamson, two remarkable Scottish photographers living in Edinburgh, produced nearly 3000 images, including city views, landscapes and scenes of everyday life. Their work undoubtedly had a profound influence on Thomson. In the years leading up to Thomson's becoming a professional photographer, photographic technology also developed at an incredible speed. The invention of the wet collodion process in 1850 is regarded as the watershed: it reduced the exposure time and the cost of making photographs; it also produced sharper images. The wet collodion process quickly replaced daguerreotype and calotype. As Thomson remarked: "the detail in wet-collodian negatives was of microscopic minuteness whilst presenting the finest gradation and printing quality which had never indeed been surpassed by any known method". But this in itself added to his difficulties: it was necessary to make the negatives on glass plates that had to be coated with wet collodion emulsion before the exposure was made, thus there was a large amount of cumbersome equipment that had to be carried from place to place.

Yet Thomson persevered. To endure hardship was part of his Victorian education. He showed enormous energy and stamina. Like many his Victorian contemporaries, he was excited by the opening up of Africa and Asia to the West, and he shared in the enthusiasm for exploring exotic places. He believed that by using photography, "the explorer may add not only to the interest, but to the permanent value of his work", and that "the camera should be a power in this age of instruction to instruct the age".

In 1862, Thomson set out for Singapore, where he opened a studio and established himself as a professional portrait photographer. Meanwhile, he also became increasingly interested in the local culture and people. From Singapore he travelled into Malaya and Sumatra and took a number of photographs of local landscapes and people. In 1866, after moving to Bangkok, he made his first photographic expedition into Cambodia and Indochina (Vietnam). His photographs of Cambodia and Siam (Thailand) established him as a serious travel photographer, and gained him membership of both the Ethnographic Society of London and the Royal Geographic Society.

During his second trip to Asia, Thomson based himself in the thriving British Crown Colony of Hong Kong in 1868. There he studied Chinese and Chinese culture while making a few short trips into Guangdong. Thomson's major China expedition began in 1870. For two years, he travelled extensively from Guangdong to Fujian, and then to eastern and northern China, including the imperial capital, Beijing, before heading down to the Yangtse river, altogether covering nearly 8000 kilometres. In China, Thomson excelled as a photographer in quality, depth and breadth, and also in artistic sensibility. The experience he gained and the techniques he developed on the streets of Beijing laid the foundation for

敦街头生活》奠定了基础。而后者不仅使汤姆逊成为了纪实摄影的先驱，也使他成为了那个时代最具影响力的摄影家之一。

汤姆逊拍摄的中国作品和维尔康姆图书馆

回到英国后，汤姆逊开始积极地向公众宣传介绍中国。除了举办图文展外，他连续发表了许多关于中国的摄影作品和文章。19世纪末，世界正在发生着翻天覆地的变化，汤姆逊洞察到了这一点。他在记录其亚洲之行的书中写道："蒸汽机和电报使中国与我们之间的关系日益紧密起来，我们不能再漠视中国"。毫无疑问，他的摄影作品使得19世纪欧洲对亚洲的认识大为改观，填补了东西方之间的视觉空白。他也获得了"中国通"的美誉。

汤姆逊作品的独到之处不仅在于其数量众多，而更重要的是他致力于忠实、准确地描绘中国的风景与人文，哪怕这种影像并不总是赏心悦目。他希望通过他的作品，观众能够目睹中国的洪水、饥馑、蝗灾和内战，他更希望通过他的作品，观众能去分享普通中国人的生活。他要求自己的作品要超越人物的格式化和群体化，而生动地描绘形形色色的芸芸众生，去捕捉每个人物的独特性。

1920年，汤姆逊决定将他拍摄的650块玻璃底版出售给维尔康姆医学史博物馆，其中包括他在中国拍摄的部分。但是这一心愿尚未完成他便与世长辞。后来，生于美国的药商和慈善家亨利·维尔康姆爵士从汤姆逊的继承人手中购买了这些底版。

虽然维尔康姆博物馆以医学和历史为主题，但亨利·维尔康姆在收藏方面的兴趣广泛，甚至到了无所不收的地步。他本人喜欢用人类学的方法来探究历史，因此想要创建一座人类博物馆，但是这个夙愿终未实现。维尔康姆去世后，三箱装有汤姆逊的底版与他的其它许多藏品一起被转送到了伦敦维尔康姆图书馆，在那里收藏至今。

本次展出的148幅影像作品就来自其中。有些照片在汤姆逊的影集中出版过或是展出过，但绝大多数作品是首次与观众见面。例如那些立体摄影系列，这些作品中的每张底版都包括两张从稍稍不同的角度拍摄的同一人或物的照片。而过去由于成本问题，一般只洗印了其中一幅。

参展照片拍摄于北京、广东和福建等地。汤姆逊在广东和福建拍摄的是他风光照片中的代表作。这些照片不仅再现了美丽的风光，同时也反映了作者的内心体验。而那些反映穷苦人民的照片更加充分地反映了作者的充满人性的同情心。从在广东和福建的拍摄开始，汤姆逊便关注着普通中国人的生活状态。随着旅程的展开，这种关怀也越发深切。从北京的照片来看，汤姆逊不但在人像摄影方面才艺卓著，他的街头摄影也是同代人中的佼佼者。在20世纪，能够拍出这样生动的街头纪实影像的大师也仅有柯特兹、布列松和杜瓦诺而已。更重要的是，这些照片是极为珍贵的历史文献。通过它们，我们可以了解19世纪末在挣扎中刚刚开始步入现代社会的中国和普通中国人的日常生活。

his *Street Life in London*, compiled five years later. This established him as the pioneer of photojournalism and one of the most influential photographers of his generation.

Thomson's China photographs and the Wellcome Library

After returning to Britain, Thomson took up an active role informing the public about China. Besides giving illustrated presentations, he continually published photographic and written works on China. He sensed that a profound transformation was taking place in the world, and "through the agency of steam and telegraphy, [China] is being brought day by day into closer relationship with ourselves...China cannot much longer lie undisturbed in *statii quo*." Undoubtedly, his photographs contributed greatly to 19th-century Europe's view of Asia and filled the visual gap between East and West. He became known as 'China' Thomson.

Yet what marked Thomson's work out was not simply the massive amount of visual information he offered. His uniqueness was his zeal to present a faithful and precise, though not always agreeable, account of China and Chinese people. He wanted his audiences to witness China's floods, famines, pestilences and civil wars; but even more so, he wanted to share with them the human aspect of life in China. He wanted his work to transcend that of the casual illustration of idiosyncratic types, to portray human beings as individuals full of peculiarities.

In 1920, Thomson decided to sell his 650 glass negatives, including those of China, to the Wellcome Historical Medical Museum, but died before the transaction could be completed. Eventually, Henry Solomon Wellcome (1853–1936), the American-born pharmacist and philanthropist, bought the negatives from Thomson's heirs.

Although Wellcome's museum had a medical and historical theme, Wellcome was a cosmopolitan and, in some aspects, compulsive collector. He also had an anthropological approach to history, and his ultimate aim was to create a Museum of Man, although he never saw this dream realized. After his death, much of his collection, including Thomson's negatives in three wooden crates, ended up in the Wellcome Library in London, where they remain today.

The 148 images included in this exhibition are all from the Wellcome Library's collection. While a few images were reproduced in Thomson's published works and shown in exhibitions, the great majority of his photographs have never been exhibited. Take, for example, the stereoscopes. Each of these negatives comprises two photographs taken from slightly different angles. Previously, due to the cost of publishing, only one of the exposures was printed.

The images included for this exhibition have been chosen mainly for their locations, namely those of Beijing, Guangdong and Fujian. The photographs Thomson took in Fujian and Guangdong are his strongest series of landscapes. But they also show his sensitivity. The human aspect of his work was even more evident in his photos of the poor. In Guangdong and Fujian he became increasingly concerned with the lives and conditions of ordinary Chinese. As he travelled farther, this concern developed. In the imperial capital of Beijing, not only did Thomson display his talent as professional portrait photographer, but also his street scenes of Beijing showed that he was ahead of his time. These deeply moving images are sometimes compared to street photographs by the great 20th-century masters such as Andre Kertesz, Henri Cartier-Bresson or Robert Doisneau. But more importantly, they will remain as incredibly valuable historical material for anyone wishing to understand 19th-century China and its people in their struggle to become modern.

大清官员毛昶熙

北京，1871-1872年，40.5×50厘米

毛昶熙（1817—1882），清末河南参陟人，字旭初。道光进士。咸丰十年（1860年）以左副都御史衔，在籍办团练围攻捻军。次年任内阁学士。同治元年（1862年）随僧格林沁在鲁、豫、鄂、皖等地镇压捻军，授礼部侍郎。先后调吏部、户部，授左都御史。八年兼署工部尚书，在总理各国事务衙门上行走。十一年改任吏部尚书。十三年兼翰林院掌院学士。光绪八年（1882年）任兵部尚书。这是汤姆逊拍摄的几张总理衙门高官中少有的没有直视镜头的官员像。

Mao Changxi (1817–1882), Minister of Foreign Affairs

Beijing, 1871–72, 40.5×50 cm

Zhongli Yamen, or the Office for Foreign Affairs, was set up in 1861 to deal with international relations and state-run modernization projects. Mao Changxi was one of the three Chinese ministers appointed for this Office, the other three being Manchu. A native of Henan, Mao entered government service through imperial exams and rose to government office of the highest rank after his success in suppressing the Taiping northern army. This is one of the very few portraits of Chinese officials taken by Thomson in which the sitter looks away from the camera.

大清官员董恂

北京，1871-1872年，84×105厘米

董恂（1810－1892），初名醇，后避同治帝讳改恂，字忱甫，号韫卿，江都县邵伯镇人。时任户部尚书。道光二十年（1840年）成进士后踏上仕宦之途，至光绪八年（1882年）正月，以高龄退休罢职，先后历事道光、咸丰、同治、光绪四朝，历任户部主事、湖南储运道、直隶清河道、顺天府尹、都察院左都御史及兵、户两部侍郎、尚书。其中户部尚书任期最长，自同治八年六月至光绪八年正月，达12年之久。在此期间曾充殿试读卷、会试正副主考官，以及文宗、穆宗二帝实录馆总裁。又曾入总理各国事务衙门，作为全权大臣，奉派与比利时、英国、俄国、美国等国签订通商条约。为维护国家利益，据理力争，不辱使命。

Dong Xun (1810–1892), Minster of Foreign Affairs

Beijing，1871–72，84×105 cm

Dong Xun was also one of the three Chinese ministers in the Office for Foreign Affairs. During his time in office, he negotiated on behalf of the Qing government, which included signing several international trade treaties with Belgium, Britain, the United States, Russia and others. Dong Xun was an extremely learned man and a prolific author. He was also a well-known authority on hydrography, and had impressed Thomson with his plans to improve irrigation and drainage throughout China.

恭亲王奕䜣肖像

北京，1871-1872年，40.5×50厘米

恭亲王奕䜣（1833－1898），道光帝六子，咸丰帝异母弟。他是咸丰、同治、光绪三朝的名王重臣，是晚清新式外交的开拓者，建议并创办了中国第一个正式外交机关。汤姆逊评价他：理解力快，广纳谏言，思想开放。这张照片拍摄于恭王府花园内的假山边。

Prince Gong (1833–1898)

Beijing, 1871–72, 40.5×50 cm

Prince Gong was the youngest brother of Emperor Xianfeng. He was little known before 1860, when the Emperor fled the capital to escape the British and French army. On behalf of his brother and the Qing government, Prince Gong met General Gordon and the allied powers and negotiated the peace treaty. After that Prince Gong held several high military and civil appointments, including membership of the Supreme Council. He was also in charge of the Office for Foreign Affairs. In this portrait Thomson intended to show a modernizer and a pro-Western figure right at the top of the Chinese government, one who was 'quick of apprehension, open to advice, and comparatively liberal in his views'.

总理衙门三满族大臣

北京，1871-1872年，50×40.5厘米

总理各国事务衙门是中国晚清主管外交事务、派出驻外国使节，并兼管通商、海防、关税、路矿、邮电、军工、同文馆、派遣留学生等事务的中央机构。初称总理各国通商事务衙门，简称总理衙门、总署或译署。三人从左往右依次为成林、宝鋆、文祥。

成林当时还不到45岁，是那时总理衙门最年轻的官员。宝鋆，字佩蘅，满洲镶白旗人，当时还任总管内务府大臣，65岁。文祥，字博川，号文山，盛京正红旗人，1861年任总理衙门大臣，后升为协办大学士、武英殿大学士等职。

Three Manchu Ministers at the Office for Foreign Affairs

Beijing, 1871–72, 50×40.5 cm

The three Manchu ministers at Office for Foreign Affairs were (from left to right) Cheng Lin, Bao Jun and Wen Xiang. Of the three, Cheng Lin was the youngest member of the Office for Foreign Affairs, being not yet more than forty-five. Bao Jun, at the age of sixty-five, was also a member of the Grand Council and one of the Presidents of the Board of Finance. Wen Xiang, born in Mukden in 1817, ranked next to Prince Gong in the Office for Foreign Affairs and had held the position since 1861. He was also a member of the Grand Council, President of the Board of Civil Service and Member of the Imperial Cabinet. A man of rare intellectual powers, coupled with his long experience in high office, Wen xiang was looked on as the most influential late Qing statesman.

晚清三大臣

北京，1871-1872年，111 × 146厘米

左侧沈桂芬，江苏吴县人，字经笙，又字小山。时任军机大臣，56岁；中间董恂，字忱甫，号韫卿，江都人。先后事道光、咸丰、同治、光绪四朝，时任户部尚书，他还是近代诗文家，同治三年(1864年)翻译美国郎费罗的《人生颂》一诗，从而成为"具体介绍近代西洋文学的第一人"(钱钟书语)，61岁；右侧为毛昶熙，时任工部尚书，56岁。他们三人同时还兼总理各国事务衙门大臣。

Three Chinese Ministers at the Office for Foreign Affairs

Beijing，1871–72，111 × 146 cm

From left to right are Shen Guifeng, Dong Xun and Mao Changxi. A native of Jiangsu, Shen Guifeng (1818–1881) was best known for his anti-opium policy and for his contributions to the state-run modernizing movement – the 'yangwu movement'. In this portrait, Thomson intended to show that Chinese officials did not spend their time in idleness and luxury, rather, they led laborious lives and dressed in simple robes. But more importantly for him these three individuals 'were as fine-looking men as ever our own Cabinet can boast. All of them had an air of quiet, dignified repose'.

清代官员

北京，1869年，112×147厘米

在大清时代，科举考试是选拔官员的一个主要途径。清代官员又分为文官和武官两大类。不同等级的官员分为九品，每品里又有正、从之分，所谓九品十八级。每个级别的官服和帽子都是不同的。汤姆逊说，正式场合，满清官员都要正襟危坐，说着正式的官话。

A Mandarin Official

Beijing, 1869, 112×147 cm

In Imperial China, a bureaucrat was called a Mandarin, who entered his office through imperial examinations. There were two types of Mandarin: those who held civil office and those awarded a military one. They were then graded into nine ranks and were distinguished by the robe and hat they wore. It was said that during the Qing, a Mandarin in public must always present himself in a stiff posture and speak in a very formal language. For many Europeans, this 'outer semblance of virtue and integrity' was thought to be rather awkward.

官员和仆役

北京，1871-1872年，42×41厘米

出现在照片中的官员在构图上虽然是传统的中国特色，包括他手中的烟斗，几上的茶杯、茶壶和茶叶盒等，但从这位官员所翘二郎腿和仆人的姿势来看，汤姆逊正努力摆脱正式的肖像拍摄方法，努力抓取人们生活中自然的一面。

A Manchu with Servant

Beijing，1871–72，42×41 cm

The man wearing spectacles and holding a pipe is dressed in Manchu outfit. He is sitting in a courtyard next to a house. Another man, apparently a servant, is standing behind. Both men wear plumed hats. There is also a Chinese-style table, with a teacup, teapot and tea-caddy on it. Here we see that Thomson, while becoming increasingly interested in the life of ordinary people, was by no means abandoning the formal portrait. The backdrop of this photo is familiar, for it appears in several street photos he took of Beijing.

正在用餐的满族妇女

北京，1871-1872年，41×40.5厘米

汤姆逊认为：总体上说，在西方人的眼里，满族妇女显得更加美丽和优雅。因为满族妇女有更大的自由度，从不裹脚。另外，他们的服饰也更加雅致。照片上六位正在用餐的满族妇女兴致各异，但站立的一老一小两个仆人则面无表情。

Manchu Ladies at Meal Table

Beijing, 1871–72, 41×40.5 cm

Thomson regarded himself extremely lucky for being admitted into 'the sacred precincts of the mysterious Chinese dwelling', where he had opportunity to gain some insights into the daily life of women in Beijing. His general impression of Manchu ladies was a positive one: they did not bind their feet as their Chinese counterparts did, thus they could enjoy more freedom. Thomson was also impressed by their grace, beauty and by their elegant and richly coloured dresses. This photograph shows a group of Manchu ladies enjoying a meal together in a courtyard.

满族新娘

北京，1871-1872年，88×85厘米

汤姆逊拍摄了大量身着盛装的满族新娘的照片，但他对这些新娘的未来生活并不乐观，甚至和奴隶制相比：富人的孩子一般比穷人的孩子结婚早，但满族少女只有到了14岁才能订婚。一般来说，人们会雇用媒婆来提早安排一桩婚事，但未来的主妇必须符合四个标准：一是要和蔼，二要文静，三要勤快，四要好看。与新娘的盛装相对照的却是她忧郁的眼神，也许这也反映了摄影师的心境。

A Manchu Bride

Beijing, 1871–72, 88×85 cm

Thomson took many photographs of Manchu brides and their magnificent wedding costumes. In this example he adopted a style that is both discreet and intimate, showing his sensitivity towards the sitter. The glimpse of sadness in her eyes reflects a gloomy view of a Manchu bride's prospects in marriage. For Thomson it was reckoned a life of slavery, in which the wife 'is even liable to be beaten by her mother-in-law, and husband too, if she neglects to discharge her duties as general domestic drudge'.

穿礼服的满族新娘和她的仆人

北京，1871-1872年，121×111厘米

根据满族的风俗，女孩只有到14岁才可以订婚。满族婚礼过程包含了各种复杂的礼仪。不过，根据家庭的经济状况，新娘的服装是清一色的红色丝绸或棉质礼服。结婚当天，新娘坐着深红色装饰的轿子到新郎家。新娘头上也会顶一块精心编制的红盖头。

A Manchu Bride in her Wedding Clothes with her Maid

Beijing，1871–72，121×111 cm

According to an old Manchu custom, a girl could not be betrothed until she was fourteen years of age. A Manchu wedding was a painstaking affair, involving numerous rituals. The bride's wedding dress would always be a simple red silk or cotton robe, depending on her family's wealth. On her wedding day, she was carried to her husband's home in a sedan chair decorated with crimson cloth. Her head was covered with a veil that was also crimson, and richly embroidered.

满族已婚女子头饰

北京，1871-1872年，41×40.5厘米

两把头是满族妇女的典型发式。两把头就是把头发束在头顶，分成两绺，在头顶上梳成一个横长式的发髻，用一根约七、八分宽，一尺来长的大横簪（又名大扁方），贯于发髻之中，再将后面的余发绾成一个燕尾式的扁髻，压在后脖领儿上。这样，发髻便无形中限制了脖颈的随便扭动，使人走起路格外庄重。汤姆逊幽默地说：也许人们会认为这长长的横簪是两个尖尖的羊角，是用来对付她们凶悍的丈夫的。

A Manchu Lady Wearing a Coiffure

Beijing, 1871–72, 41×40.5 cm

A Manchu coiffure differed widely from a Chinese one and it therefore became a marker of ethnic difference among women. Represented here is the coiffure of a married Manchu lady. The basis of this coiffure consists of a flat strip of wood, ivory or precious metal about a foot in length. Half of the real hair of the wearer is gathered up and twisted in broad bands around this support, which is then laid across the back of the head. Thomson was intrigued by this simple, graceful yet strange-looking headdress, he thought it 'must have been designed, to represent horns . . . enabling the wearer to hold her own against her antagonistic husband'.

满族已婚女子头饰

北京，1871-1872年，88×86厘米

满族的妇女历来就非常讲究头饰，除了用于固定发髻和头型的实用簪，像这位妇女头饰上还用了装饰簪，它们都被戴在明显的位置上，更显得富贵华丽。另外，这位妇女上身所穿的做工精美的绣花上衣，也是吸引约翰逊拍摄的一个重要原因。

A Seated Manchu Lady Wearing a Coiffure

Beijing, 1871–72, 88×86 cm

Thomson was fascinated by the different types of female coiffure in China. This coiffure worn by another married Manchu lady was a trademark Manchu hairstyle in the late Qing. It required the hair to be wrapped up in an elaborate triangular pattern around a wood, ivory or metal fillet fastened behind the head. When completed, a coiffure extended out at the back as well as to both sides. Flowers or tassels were often attached to the coiffure to make it more impressive.

室内站立的满族男子

北京，1871-1872年，40.5×42厘米

男子身着特色满族长袍，头顶貂皮帽，并戴着眼镜。从服饰可以判断出他非富即贵，背景中还隐约可见他的仆人。当时眼镜是很时髦的舶来品，也是人们财富和地位的象征。这种侧脸照相姿势并不是中国人的传统，男子努力想直视镜头，一定是汤姆逊导演所致。

A Standing Manchu Official

Beijing, 1871–72, 40.5×42 cm

This man wears a Manchu-style silk robe, a hat and spectacles, an outfit that suggests he is of some wealth and the holder of an official rank. The foreign spectacles further convey his prestige. In China, photos were always related to wealth and status. Thus like this man, most people looked straight at camera and were photographed in full. Clothes offered visual evidence of a man's worth, while full body photograph captured a larger part of the all-important backdrop. Furthermore, because funeral portraits were always half-length, a general taboo developed in which half-length photographs were deemed unsuitable for the living.

室内端坐的满族男子

北京，1871-1872年，41×41厘米

在这张照片中，满族男子坐了下来，并摆出了中国人传统的照相姿势。比较汤姆逊拍摄的中国其他高官的照片，没有一张侧面照片，全部是直视镜头的，并且是全身照。由此可以判断出，此男子的社会地位远远低于其他高官，才有可能被汤姆逊导演拍摄了另外那张站立侧面肖像。

A Seated Manchu Official

Beijing，1871–72，41×41 cm

Here is the Manchu official, sitting on a chair next to a Chinese-style table. On the table is a teacup. This arrangement of small table, teacup and simple backdrop appears repeatedly in Thomson's portraits of the mandarin class in China. This official's foreign spectacles are juxtaposed with the furnishings: while sipping tea, he, like many men of status in China, is looking to the West and to modernization.

买头饰的满族妇女

北京，1871-1872年，41×40.5厘米

北京的满族妇女十分重视头饰。作为一种戴在头上的首饰，不仅起到美饰发髻的作用，还有托物寄情、表达心声意愿的美好追求。从照片中满族妇女的穿着来看，应当是富贵人家的妇女，而贩卖头饰在当时的北京一定是个很赚钱的行当。

Manchu Women Buying Flowers for Their Headdress

Beijing，1871–72，41×40.5 cm

As an ethnic mark of identity, the headdress played an important part in the life of a Manchu bannerwoman. While still a girl, she would wear a single pigtail hanging behind, with the front hair cut into a fringe. After marriage, however, she must arrange the hair on the top of the head and put a fan-shaped hair coronet on the arrangement. This hairstyle is called 'Qitou' (which means hair for the Manchu nobility) or 'Jingtou' (which means hair of the capital). Many women also liked to wear flower-press hair ornaments made of gold, silver or emerald.

满族杨氏家族女眷

北京，1871-1872年，40.5×41厘米

在汤姆逊的北京之行中，他和一个姓杨的中国富商成为好友，从而得以被邀请到他家里参观。这位姓杨的富商喜欢收集外国的照相设备，自己还亲手实践摄影。汤姆逊被富商家中美丽的庭院所震撼，在假山前拍摄了这名满族女子的照片。照片中女子的美丽和温顺与后面的石山形成了鲜明的对比，正像汤姆逊所说，这些女子整天身处深宅大院当中，对庭院外的世界一无所知。

Young Woman Standing in a Rock Garden

Beijing，1871–72，40.5 × 41 cm

During his visit to Beijing, Thomson was befriended by a rich local gentleman, a certain Mr Yang. Like many of his wealthy contemporaries, Yang aspired to things foreign. He became particularly interested in collecting photographic equipment. His curiosity and genuine kindness allowed Thomson to enter his home and obtain a glimpse of the domestic life, especially of women. Here a young woman stands in a rock garden. Like most women of well-off families, she lived a life of seclusion, knowing little or nothing of the world beyond the walls of what can be seen to be a beautiful courtyard house.

庭院里的满族和汉族女子

北京，1871-1872年，42×40.5厘米

这是在杨方家的院子里拍摄的，三个女人一个面对镜头，一个背对镜头，另一个是侧对镜头。汤姆逊很显然是想展示三个女人的发式。汤姆逊说：坦白地讲，我自己都不能解释这复杂的发式究竟是如何完成的。根据坐着的女子的小脚和发式看，她是汉族女子。

Manchu and Chinese Ladies inside a Courtyard

Beijing, 1871–72, 42×40.5 cm

We are in Mr Yang's courtyard. One woman faces the camera, another stands with her back towards the camera, while the Chinese with bound feet sits sideways. Clearly, in this photograph Thomson wished not only to show the Chinese woman's golden lilies (euphemism for bound feet) but also to show the elaborate hairstyles of Manchu women: 'I confess myself unable to explain the mysterious mode in which the tresses have been twisted, but careful study of the illustrations will, I doubt not, reward any lady who may desire to dress her hair "a la Manchu"'.

满族妇人和女佣

北京，1871-1872年，40.5×45厘米

这是北京杨方家的女子，身着华丽的绸缎服装在堆满假山的花园中。根据汤姆逊的纪录，西方人更喜欢满族妇女的美丽和优雅。在赞赏她们的小脚的同时，汤姆逊还充分肯定了她们优雅的长袍："颜色丰富、优雅，夏天明亮，冬天温暖，和天气很搭配"。

A Manchu Lady with her Maid

Beijing，1871–72，40.5×45 cm

This female member of Mr Yang's family dressed in rich satin outfit is standing with her maid in a rocky garden. According to Thomson, Manchu ladies, in terms of beauty and grace, appeared more pleasing to the Western eye. While admiring their unbound, naturally small feet, he also praised their robes as always elegant: 'The full robes of a lady . . . of the wealthier classes are highly picturesque and remarkable also for the richness and beauty of their materials. The costume is ample, graceful and well adapted to the climate, light in summer and warm enough in winter.'

正在梳妆的满族女子

北京，1871-1872年，120×112厘米

在杨方先生家里，汤姆逊拍摄了满族女子梳妆的详细过程。整理头发也许是这个过程中最重要的一环，通常需要仆人用一两个小时的时间来完成。"很多人使用假头髻和假发，但不用染发剂"。整个画面充满了温情与平和，也应当是汤姆逊人道主义情怀在拍摄时的一个典型体现。照片中不论是温情的女主人，还是笃厚的侍女或者无邪的孩童，都带给我们一种阳光的温暖，让我们暂时忘掉了当时正摇摇欲坠的大清帝国和一个腐朽没落的政权。

A Manchu Lady having her Hair dressed by Servant Girl

Beijing, 1871–72, 120×112 cm

At Mr Yang's home, Thomson had the opportunity to observe the detailed – often tedious – routines of a Manchu lady being dressed by her servant girl. Hairdressing perhaps constituted the most important part of the day for a Manchu lady. In general it took one to two hours for the servant to dress her lady's hair: 'Many of them have chignons and false hair; but no hair-dyes are used, for raven hair is common and golden tresses are not in repute.'

满族妇女和她的儿媳及孙辈

北京，1871-1872年，42.5×41厘米

在中国，一个家族的大小是一种社会声望的标志，家族的合影在当时就受到了人们的欢迎，这种合影也体现一个家族的社会认同。从照片上看，这位略带微笑的妇人对生活还是满足的。

A Manchu Lady with her Daughter in-law and Grandchildren

Beijing，1871–72，42.5×41 cm

In China, photographs are at the core of the social representation of identity. With lineage provides an overarching sense of identity, family portraits are particularly popular, as family size is a matter of social prestige. The lady in the photograph is looking content with her daughter in-law and three grandchildren by her side.

满族妇女和她的儿媳

北京，1871-1872年，41×41厘米

从不同眼神或许能够看出两个人不同的社会地位。汤姆逊观察到，直视镜头的婆婆在家庭大事中拥有绝对的权力。而站立的儿媳不仅要侍奉好丈夫，还要看婆婆的眼色行事。如果婆婆是个狠心的女人，那年轻的媳妇第一年的新婚生活就会像奴隶一样。

A Manchu Lady with her Daughter-in-law

Beijing, 1871–72, 41×41 cm

In this photograph the older woman stares straight into the camera, while the younger one looks away and slightly down. Their attitudes indicate their social position. As Thomson observed, in a Manchu household the mother-in-law held absolute authority over the domestic scene. A Manchu daughter-in-law not only had to serve her husband diligently, she was also constantly watched over by her mother-in-law. If the mother-in-law was a hard-hearted woman, the young wife might spend the first years of her married life in a state of slavery.

满族妇女和她的儿媳

北京，1871-1872年，40 × 52厘米

这是满族妇女和儿媳的全身照。就像她们两个的半身照一样，婆婆显得很严肃，但在和孙子们的照片里，她则是微笑的。在所有三张照片里，媳妇的眼睛都是看一侧的，这也说明了她在婆婆面前的地位。在这张照片里，汤姆逊似乎还试图向人们展示满族妇女的天足。

A Manchu Lady with her Daughter in-law

Beijing，1871–72，40 × 52 cm

This is a full-length portrait of the same Manchu lady with her daughter-in-law. In this photograph, as well as in the half-length portrait with her daughter-in-law, the elderly lady looked rather severe, whereas in the photograph with her grandchildren, she smiles at the camera. In all three images the daughter-in-law looks sideways, suggesting her low position in front of her mother-in-law. In this particular image, it was also likely that Thomson also tried to illustrate the unbound natural feet of Manchu ladies.

满族妇女和孩子

北京，1871-1872年，41.5×40.5厘米

在一个传统庭院的屏风前，汤姆逊拍摄了这张妇女和儿童相对的照片。妇女精心的头饰和美丽的丝绸长袍，都吸引了汤姆逊。汤姆逊之所以拍摄她全身的侧面肖像，就是想展现"中国上层社会的妇女或男子长袍是很独特的，衣料华美而又充满质感"。

A Manchu Lady with a Child

Beijing，1871–72，41.5×40.5 cm

The woman and the child face one another in front of a screen inside a courtyard. The woman wears an elaborate hairstyle and a beautiful silk robe. They are photographed at full length in part because Thomson wanted to show that 'the full robes of a Chinese lady or gentleman of the better classes are highly picturesque, and remarkable also for the richness and beauty of their materials'.

铜香炉边的满族女子和仆人

北京，1871-1872年，40.5×40.5厘米

老仆人右手拿着水烟袋，左手被她的主人抓扶着。在满族妇女中，吸烟已经成为很受欢迎的消遣方式，不仅仅是为了打发时间，也是当时的一种社交方式。虽然有很多人吸食鸦片，但更多人是吸水烟。在北京炎热的夏季，吸烟也是一种消夏的选择。

A Manchu Lady with her Maid standing beside a Bronze Burner

Beijing, 1871–72, 40.5×40.5 cm

This Manchu lady stands next to a bronze burner with her elderly maid. The lady gazes full face at the camera, while the maid's head is turned slightly away. The maid holds the lady's water-pipe in her right hand, while her left hand is held by her mistress. Smoking was a popular pastime among Manchu women, not only to divert boredom, but because it was considered to be a sociable activity. Although many people smoked opium, the water-pipe was more widely available; it was also a more soothing choice on a hot summer's day.

铜炉边的满族妇女和女仆

北京，1871-1872年，44.5×41厘米

在这张图片里，女仆直视镜头，而女主人则旁看他侧。这说明，汤姆逊试图改变传统正式的肖像拍摄模式。同时也表明，当时的满族女仆更像女主人的一个玩伴。虽然她需要为主人梳妆、穿衣和讨好她，但女仆不必干任何重活，女仆还可以使唤主人别的丫鬟。

A Manchu Woman with her Maid standing beside a Bronze Burner

Beijing, 1871–72, 44.5×41 cm

Here, while the maid stares straight at the camera, her mistress looks askance, suggesting that Thomson was trying to move away from the formal portrait tradition, attempting to portray his subjects as individuals. It also shows he was trying to convey the ambiguous role of a Manchu maid: she was more like a companion to her lady. Although she would dress and amuse her lady, she did not do any hard labour, and was waited on by the lady's servant girl.

化妆后的满族女子

北京，1871-1872年，40.5×41厘米

满族女子在梳理完头发后，开始化妆脸部。在清代，不论是满族还是汉族女子，尤其是富裕人家的女子，喜欢用一层厚厚的白粉来覆盖脸部和颈部。当这层粉变干后，就会显得皮肤光滑和明亮。然后，妇女们又会给脸颊打点腮红和眼影。画面中的满族妇女好像对自己的化妆效果还比较满意。

A Manchu Lady after having her Face Painted

Beijing，1871–72，40.5×41 cm

After the hair had been dressed, the face was painted. In Qing China, Manchu and Chinese women, in particular those from wealthy families, tended to cover both their face and neck with a thick white paste. When the paste was dry, it was smoothed and polished once. Afterwards a blush of rose-powder was applied to the cheeks and eyelids, with the surplus rouge left on the lady's palms, as rose-pink on the hand was greatly esteemed.

教会学校

北京，1871-1872年，40×41厘米

清末北京的教会学校主要是为了培养外语人才。很多中国孩子在这里学到基本外语知识后，成为了翻译、买办、或外国公司的职员。当时北京有大量外国商业或政务活动，需要一批既了解本地状况又通晓外语的人才，但相对外国雇员来说，这些中国孩子学成后从事的都是低端的工作。

Mission School

Beijing, 1871-72, 40×41 cm

Modern education did not begin in China until 1905. Although in Beijing, as well as in some coastal areas, there were already a number of privately run missionary schools. With few exceptions, or instance, those run by Jesuits, the majority of these were at elementary level and devoted entirely to instruction in religion and Chinese classics. This situation only began to change after 1877. During the Protestant general conference that year, it was agreed that China's mission schools were to provide a secular education, although text-books with secular contents did not appear until as late as 1890. This change made it possible for a number of ordinary Chinese to receive a Western secular education.

磨刀工

北京，1871-1872年，42×40.5厘米

汤姆逊拍摄了大量北京街头生活的照片。他在说明中描述当时的北京街道时说：当中凸起的道路可以供两辆手推车并排通过，街道两旁是林立的商店，在商店和手推车道路之间的空地上，布满了各种商亭、货摊、帐篷等流动商贩，这些流动商贩构成了老北京一道独特的风景。

A Knife-grinder

Beijing，1871–72 ，42×40.5 cm

The street remained a place of fascination for Thomson and the 'street life' of both Asia and London occupied a central place in his work. As the capital of the Qing Empire, Beijing and its streets were described by Thomson as 'highly picturesque and interesting'. People formed an essential part of this picturesque charm, particularly the traders and artisans who plied their skills and wares along the streets. This photograph of a travelling knife-grinder reveals that his work-bench was also a cart, which he pushed around little hutongs, looking for customers.

景泰蓝制作

北京，1871-1872年，40.5×40.5厘米

这是汤姆逊拍摄的北京制作景泰蓝的画面，汤姆逊了解到了景泰蓝的制作过程，并详细地记录下来。这家作坊的老板是满族人，位于东交民巷法国使馆的不远处。整个画面构图并不饱满，很有可能是当时的艺人为了保密，并没有给汤姆逊更多拍摄机会的缘故。

Enamellers

Beijing，1871–72，40.5×40.5 cm

In late Qing, there was a sudden craze for enamelware, which could fetch a very high prices in the market-place. However the art of making enamelware was becoming a rare skill, with only one or two shops in Beijing managing to carry on the tradition. This shop shown in this photograph was owned by a Manchu. It was situated not far from the French Legation quarter in Dongjiao minxiang. The workers here are rather boyish-looking but Thomson was very impressed by their expert skills in colour-blending.

修脚师

北京，1871-1872年，43×40.5厘米

这些修脚师不单单可以提供剪剪脚指甲等简单的服务，同时他们还是一个流动的脚医，可以根治鸡眼等各种脚病。整个画面生动有趣，把修脚师的认真、顾客的信任表现得淋漓尽致。尤其是从破败的门窗上伸出头的老者，口含大烟斗，平静地欣赏修脚师的技艺，为整幅照片增加了几丝情趣。

A Travelling Chiropodist

Beijing，1871–72，43×40.5 cm

Until the advent of modern medicine, most people in China sought help from quack doctors and herbal remedies for their ailments. In late Qing, the streets of major cities were full of quacks, many of whom also practised as barbers and ear-cleaners. Here an itinerant chiropodist is operating on a painful corn and dressing the toe-nails of his patient. A second customer leaning out of a dilapidated window patiently waits his turn, while smoking a pipe of peace.

卖水果的商贩

北京，1871-1872年，43×40.5厘米

这是当时老北京走街串巷卖时令水果的商贩，汤姆逊说：商贩把商店扛在了自己的肩膀上。他在狭窄的胡同里，挨家挨户地推销上等的葡萄。摄影师拍摄的是他叫卖时的精彩一瞬，一个孩子低头看着令人垂涎欲滴的葡萄，使画面平添几分生动。

A Travelling Fruit-seller

Beijing, 1871–72, 43 × 40.5 cm

In imperial Beijing, shop-owners and travelling salesmen were mainly Chinese or Muslims (although despite the shared business culture, the latter were considered to be lower down the social scale). They carried their 'shop' on their shoulders, walking from street to street while calling out to advertise their wares. Unlike today, back then it was the customer who had his own weighing machine to hand to ensure he received the amount he was paying for. Here a fruitseller is calling out to would-be customers that he has brought to their doors the choicest grapes of the season.

拾荒者

北京，1871-1872年，41×40.5厘米

这位衣衫褴褛的老者主要是捡拾地上的纸片，另外，他也到处寻找破布头和各种骨头，他会每天把这些东西卖给收购者。他看起来贫穷悲惨，甚至没有家庭和朋友，但依靠劳动生存，赢得了汤姆逊的尊重。

Rag and Bone Man

Beijing，1871–72，41×40.5 cm

Beijing's streets were once full of collectors who made their living picking up any kind of recyclable items, from bits of coal to scraps of paper and used cloth. The majority of such collectors were children and the elderly. They would hang around for other people or the state-run carts to dump their rubbish, whereupon they fought to get anything they might be able to sell for a pittance. This old man made his living by collecting scraps of printed paper money, offerings that were manufactured in order to be burned before shrines. He also gathered rags and bones from the rubbish heaps, selling his miscellany to a dealer at the end of each weary day.

观看西洋景

北京，1871-1872年，41.5×40.5厘米

西洋景又称“拉洋片”，是清末北京街头很受欢迎的一种娱乐方式。在电影尚未传入中国和普及的年代，西洋景是一种代替电影的娱乐方式，堪称中国独有的街头“土电影”。表演时艺人将各种图画装入特制的大木箱中，箱子外壁设若干小孔，孔中装凸镜，观看者通过凸镜往箱内观看。表演者一边拉放画片，一边根据画面内容配以唱词和锣鼓。

‘Magic lantern’ Peep Show

Beijing, 1871–72, 41.5×40.5 cm

Slide or ‘magic lantern’ shows were a novelty in China in the late 1860s. The lantern was considered ‘truly ingenious beyond belief’ and it soon attracted a mass popular audience. People in China who had never travelled could learn about foreign places through the slide show, discovering the world beyond the confines of their home village or region. Often a showman delivered a running commentary on the mysterious scenes as he introduces them, sometimes there was even music accompaniment. To attract customers, many presenters also included a few images of naked women in the middle or at the end of a show.

出殡旗手

北京，1871-1872年，42×40.5厘米

满族葬礼过程经过精心设计，花费很多，有的棺材是64人所抬，称六十四杠。汤姆逊从一个传教士那里了解到了满族葬礼的过程，照片上的人都是参加葬礼的旗手，叫做打执手的，他们都是被临时雇用的乞丐。满族人和汉族人葬礼所用的旗帜和器具有很大的差别。每一个满族旗人的葬礼都会从政府那里得到些补贴来弥补葬礼的花费。

Hired Bannermen in a Manchu Funeral Procession

Beijing，1871–72，42×40.5 cm

A Manchu funeral procession in imperial China was an extremely elaborate and costly affair. Sometimes the coffin would be carried by as many as 64 men; the canopy covering it was often decorated with embroidered white satin. Wailing household women would follow the procession in carts covered with white material. Bannermen, commonly beggars, were hired to take part. The banners and paraphernalia were integral parts of a Manchu funeral and they differed greatly from the ornaments used in a Chinese one. The Qing government gave an allowance towards the costs of Manchu funerals.

锔碗匠

北京，1871-1872年，41×40.5厘米

在北京的街道上，各种工匠把大街上的空地占满了。画面上这个人正在把一个盘子递给锔碗匠。当时很多人家如果碰到家里的水缸、碗、盆或盘子裂开或打碎了，都会找锔碗匠用金属丝锔上继续使用。

A Mender of Broken Chinaware

Beijing, 1871–72, 41 × 40.5 cm

During his visit to Beijing, Thomson noted that artisans plied their trades on every vacant space in the streets of the city. Here, one man is standing while holding a plate, the other, the mender, is sitting with a yoke and panniers.A boy stands behind them, looking away.

街边古董摊

北京，1871-1872年，120×111厘米

就像很多来到北京的外国人一样，汤姆逊有一天在大街上被六七个古董商围住，通过他在天津雇佣的仆人向他推销古董。汤姆逊也确实购买了一些。更重要的是，购买完后，他拍摄了这幅图画，为我们保留下了珍贵的资料。

A Dealer of Curiosities

Beijing, 1871–72, 120×111 cm

Even in the second half of the 19th century, foreign visitors were a regular target for antiques dealers, who tended to charge very high prices. One evening Thomson found himself waited on by a dozen such dealers, who sought to sell him old porcelain bowls, dishes and various other items at exorbitant prices. The dealers were introduced to him by a servant he had previously employed. It was a common practice for household servants to introduce dealers to foreigners, for the servants received half of the profits.

更夫

北京，1871-1872年，40.5×40.5厘米

打更在中国是一门古老的职业。更夫每天夜里敲竹梆子或锣，提醒人们现在是什么时间，也有提醒人们防火、防盗的功能。这位姓王的旗人身穿破羊皮袄，手持竹梆，张大嘴巴估计在喊：关好门窗，小心火烛！他是在北京一所法国旅馆工作的更夫。

Old Wang, a Night Watchman

Beijing，1871–72，40.5×40.5 cm

In Imperial China, people relied on night watchmen or gatekeepers to tell them the time and to keep an eye out for thieves. Many were employed by the government to ensure general security in cities and villages. Most watchmen carried a wooden clapper, as seen in this photograph, which the watchmen used to announce their presence and scare away thieves. This watchman is an old Manchu bannerman. Known as 'old Wang', he was the night gatekeeper of a French-owned hotel. Wrapping his sheepskin coat over underclothes that were little more than rags, old Wang lay through the cold nights on the stone steps of the outer gateway, only rousing himself to answer the occasional calls of his fellow watchmen nearby.

母亲和两个孩子

北京，1871-1872年，40×44厘米

汤姆逊把当时北京的街道形容为：很独特和有趣。大街上的人是他关注的主要对象，在汤姆逊的很多作品中都表现出他对穷苦百姓的极大同情。汤姆逊在前门附近的一个肉铺前遇到了这个抱孩子的妇女，她穿着朴素，但衣服很干净得体，肯定不是富裕之家的人。

Mother with Two Children

Beijing，1871–72，40×44 cm

Thomson described the streets of Beijing as 'highly picturesque and interesting' and the people formed an essential part of its charm. In many works he betrayed a great deal of sympathy towards the poor. Here a woman is holding a child in her arms. Next to her, looking away from the camera, stands a boy eating a piece of pastry. Thomson met them in front of a butcher's shop while touring the Qianmen area of the city. They are dressed in plain but warm and clean clothing, outfits that indicate they are not from a wealthy family.

老人和他的骡子

北京，1871-1872年，42.5×40.5厘米

当时的北京，骡子是一种最主要的交通工具了，汤姆逊认为北京的骡子"很聪敏和有耐性"。骡子不仅用来运输货物，同时还可以把人们运到长城。实际上，汤姆逊去长城就是依靠两只骡子组成的"骡轿"到达的。

An Old Man with his Mule

Beijing, 1871–72, 42.5×40.5 cm

As Thomson noted, the mule was a leading means of transportation within and beyond Beijing, and over time he had formed 'a high opinion of the sagacity and patience of Pekingese mules'. They were used not only for carrying goods, but to ferry people up to the Great Wall. Thomson himself was in fact carried up to the Wall by a Beijing-style mule litter.

骆驼和主人

北京，1871-1872年，120×111厘米

在现代交通工具铁路使用之前，骆驼是老北京主要的对外运输工具之一，它们把粮食和煤炭运到城区，同时把茶叶运到蒙古、俄罗斯等地。骆驼和其他动物不一样，特别耐饥耐渴。它的驼峰里贮存着脂肪，这些脂肪在骆驼得不到食物的时候，能够分解成养分以供身体之需。

A Camel with its Owner

Beijing, 1871–72, 120 × 111 cm

Until the advent of the railways, camel was the main form of transportation throughout north China and into Central Asia. This animal was held in high esteem among the Mongols, for it is physically adapted for traversing the sandy plains of the Gobi Desert. The camel's stomach has bladders that enable it to carry a store of fresh water, and its humps are furnished with a store of food in the shape of fatty matter that can be absorbed in times of need.

出发到莫斯科的驼队

北京，1871-1872年，42.5×41厘米

汤姆逊曾经亲眼看见一个由2000只骆驼组成的驼队，背负着茶砖，准备运到俄罗斯。在内蒙古戈壁大漠上，时常可以看见由成千上万只骆驼组成的奔赴俄罗斯的商队。茶砖是当时蒙古、西伯利亚和中国西藏地区主要的物物交换商品。当然，这些骆驼有时也会被雇用来运输煤炭和其它商品。

Camels Carrying Brick Tea Departing for Russia

Beijing, 1871–72, 42.5×41 cm

On one occasion Thomson watched the departure of 2,000 of these camels laden with brick tea that was to be sold in the Russian markets. At certain seasons of the year, tea-laden camels could be encountered in their tens of thousands crossing the Gobi Desert to Russia. This brick tea, in the absence of a metal currency, was the means of barter and exchange in Mongolia, Siberia and Tibet. In addition to tea, camels were also employed to transport coal and other commodities.

蒙古帐篷

北京，1871-1872年，42×40.5厘米

每年冬天，大批的蒙古人会到北京，他们携带来大量的牲畜、冰冻的野味，还有皮货。当时在东郊民巷英国大使馆的后面，已经自发形成了一个交易市场，很多蒙古人搭起帐篷，暂时居住在那里。

A Mongol Tent

Beijing, 1871–72, 42×40.5 cm

Every winter in imperial China, a great number of Mongols travelled to Beijing, bringing with them herds of cattle, quantities of frozen game, and to rich furs. At the back of the British Legation in Dongjiao minxiang, there was a market where the Mongols gathered to set up their tents.

蒙古女人和她的马

北京，1871-1872年，41.5×40.5厘米

蒙古族习惯了以游牧为生。汤姆逊遇到的这家蒙古家庭在北京租房居住，但令汤姆逊感到意外的是，他们把自家的骡子养在屋里，自己却住在院子中搭起的帐篷里。很显然，这是当时在北京的很多蒙古人的做法。

An Old Mongol Woman with her Horse

Beijing, 1871–72, 41.5×40.5 cm

Mongols are nomads at heart. This old Mongol lady's family, whom Thomson met, rented a house in Beijing. To his surprise he found that the family stabled their mules in the dwelling-house proper, while they set up their tents lived in the courtyard. Apparently this was a common practice among Mongols visiting Beijing at the time.

穆斯林屠户

北京，1871-1872年，40.5×41.5厘米

清代北京的肉铺有汉人经营的，也有穆斯林经营的。但人们觉得穆斯林经营的肉质更好，切割更熟练。照片中的肉铺位于前门地区，汤姆逊说，这位屠户有着一张快乐、微笑的脸，站在木制的小柜台后面，“四周被羊的肢体、可怕的头颅和内脏所包围”。

A Muslim Butcher

Beijing, 1871–72, 40.5×41.5 cm

Throughout the Qing, Beijing's butcher shops were run by the Chinese and Muslims. Muslim butchers, in particular, were known for their good-quality meat and carving skills. The man in this photograph had a shop in the Qianmen area. According to Thomson, he had a happy, smiling face, and stood behind a small wooden counter 'encircled by carcasses of sheep, ghastly heads, and entrails'.

老年穆斯林厨师和他的助手

北京，1871-1872年，41.5×41厘米

除了卖肉外，很多穆斯林也在北京经营便宜的小吃摊。这位照片中的老者就在前门有一个小吃棚。他的小吃棚前面摆着几个砖炉和壁炉，从那里不时飘出烤肉的香味。这个小吃摊主要做馅饼，老者负责填充制作，年轻人负责和面。

An Old Muslim Cook with his Assistant

Beijing，1871–2，41.5 × 41 cm

In addition to being butchers, Muslims also ran a number of cheap eating houses and bakeries in Beijing. The older man shown here had a small cook's shed in Qianmen area. In front of his shop was a series of brick ovens and fire-places, from these a pungent aroma of roasting spread constantly. The shop specialized in various baked and stuffed bread with both savoury meat and sweet fillings. While the older man presided over the cooking and stuffing the bread, his assistant rolled the dough.

孔庙大成殿内景

北京，1871-1872年，40.5×40.5厘米

北京孔庙是中国元、明、清三朝祭祀孔子的场所，位于北京东城区国子监街。大成殿是整座孔庙的中心建筑，大殿内外高悬清康熙至宣统九位皇帝的御匾，均是皇帝亲书的对孔子的四字赞语。"万世师表"是康熙帝御书，意为孔夫子永远是人们的老师，现在这块匾额已经悬挂在大成殿外了。

The Great Perfection Hall at the Temple of Confucius

Beijing, 1871–72, 40.5 × 40.5 cm

Situated next to the ancient National University, or Guozijian, the Temple of Confucius was a shrine where people paid homage to Confucius throughout the Yuan, Ming and Qing Dynasties. The Great Perfection Hall, situated in the centre of the Temple, is one of the most imposing examples of imperial architecture in Beijing. Both inside and outside the Hall, there are inscriptions by nine Qing emperors added since the time of Kangxi emperor. The large, gold-lettered inscription above the Hall, by Kangxi emperor, reads 'The teacher and example of ten thousand generations'.

国子监琉璃牌坊

北京，1871-1872年，50×41厘米

北京国子监是元、明、清三代的最高学府，建于元大德十年（1306年）。位于国子监二门内这座三洞式的黄色琉璃瓦牌坊建于乾隆四十八年（1783年），高大秀丽，坊壁雕飞舞盘龙，正中楼南面书额镌刻“圜桥教泽”，北面是“学海节观”。为三间四柱七楼庑殿顶式，是北京唯一一座专为教育而设的牌坊，也是中国古代崇文重教的象征。

Tiled Triple Archway, or Honorary Portal, National University

Beijing, 1871–72, 50×41 cm

Guozijian, or the National University, was the highest national learning institution throughout three dynasties – the Yuan, the Ming and the Qing. It was established in 1306 and includes this stunning triple archway or honorary portal. The roof is covered entirely with yellow glazed tiles. This is the only archway in Beijing erected to honour education, announcing that, in imperial China, learning and knowledge hold a central place. There are inscriptions by the Qianlong emperor on both sides of the archway.

大高殿牌坊

北京，1871-1872年，42×41厘米

大高殿又称大高玄殿，是明清两代皇家道观。建于明嘉靖二十一年（1542年），位于西城区景山前街。该殿坐北朝南，大高殿门外有东、西、南三座牌坊，均为四柱九楼。照片中为西牌坊，匾额正面镌“弘佑天民”，背面镌“太极仙林”。1949年后原牌楼已移至中共中央党校，现在院内“掠燕湖”的北岸。

Pailou at Dagao Hall

Beijing，1871–72，42×41 cm

In imperial China, any man might obtain permission from the emperor to erect a pailou or honorary portal in honour of himself, his children or his deceased parents. This example was originally situated outside of Daoist Dagao Temple in the north of the Forbidden City. It was built by the Jiajing Emperor in 1542, who came here seeking immortality. In the years that followed, various emperors from Ming to Qing visited Dagao Hall in order to pray for rain. After 1949 this particular pailou was relocated to the northwest of Beijing, by Lake Lue-Yan.

清漪园宝云阁

北京，1871-1872年，111 × 136厘米

宝云阁位于北京清漪园（1888年改名颐和园）万寿山上，建于清乾隆二十年（1755年）。外观似一座四方亭子，因全部用铜铸成，故又称“金殿”。外形仿照木结构建筑的样式，重檐歇山顶。清朝统治时期，西藏喇嘛到达北京，常来这里念经祈祷，举行参拜仪式。1860年，英法联军火焚清漪园，铜亭幸免于难，是清漪园中为数不多的幸存建筑之一。

Ruins of Bronze Temple in the Garden of Clear Ripple

Beijing，1871–72，111 × 136 cm

The Bronze Temple was one of the most impressive buildings on Longevity Hill within the Summer Palace, previously known as the Garden of Clear Ripple. Formally called Cloud Dispelling Hall, the Temple was first built in 1755 at the foot of Longevity Hill. It was, according to Thomson,'a very perfect example of Chinese temple architecture, showing, as it does, the most minute details of construction, and the skill with which the Chinese can work in metals, and adapt them to almost every use'. In the following years, the Temple was used for prayer whenever the Tibetan Lama visited the imperial capital. It thus contained numerous Buddhist objects made of bronze, including a statue of Siddhattha Gotama. Although many of these items were taken by the French and British in 1860, the building itself survived.

清漪园之众香界和智慧海

北京，1871-1872年，50×41厘米

众香界和智慧海在清漪园佛香阁的北面山坡上。众香界是一座砖筑琉璃贴面作装饰的牌楼。智慧海是一座全部结构用砖造的建筑，建在万寿山的最高处，殿内供有观音和菩萨像，外墙全部用黄绿二色琉璃包身，上面排满了琉璃小佛像。由于两建筑无木料，故1860年未被烧毁，是清漪园中得以幸存的建筑之一。

The Sea of Wisdom Temple, the Garden of Clear Ripple

Beijing，1871-72，50×41 cm

The Sea of Wisdom Temple, also known as the 'hall without beams', is a religious building on top of Longevity Hill. Its name indicates that the Buddha's wisdom is as wide as the sea. First built in the latter half of the 18th century, its construction was undertaken without the use of either columns or beams and it is faced entirely with glazed tiles. The original external decoration also included 1,100 small, glazed Buddhist sculptured tiles, but although the Temple survived the looting of 1860, many of the golden Buddhist sculptures swathed in the tiles were damaged.

清漪园之大报恩延寿寺遗址

北京，1871年，51×40.5厘米

大报恩延寿寺在万寿山前建筑的中心部位，原是乾隆为他母亲六十寿辰而建，1860年被英法联军焚毁。从此照片中还依稀可以看出当年的原貌。1888年慈禧重建时改为排云殿，是慈禧在园内居住和过生日时接受朝拜的地方，现在这组建筑是颐和园最为壮观的建筑群体。

Ruins of the Sculptured Terrace, Longevity Hill, the Garden of Clear Ripple

Beijing，1871，51×40.5 cm

The Garden of Clear Ripple was first laid out in 1750 under the Qianlong Emperor and was completed in 1764. The Garden encompassed the architectural styles of various palaces throughout China, while its artificial lake was modelled on the West Lake in Hangzhou, and was named as Kunming Lake in an attempt to associate it with the artificial lake built by Emperor Wu of the Han Dynasty. The Longevity Hill standing in the centre of the Garden was over 60 metres high and was built entirely using the earth excavated to make the Lake. The name 'Longevity' Hill was given by the Emperor in celebration of his mother's birthday. In 1860 the Garden was looted and torched by British and French troops during the Arrow War. In 1886 the Empress Cixi ordered its restoration, renaming it the Garden of Nurtured Harmony. As her new summer resort, the Garden of Nurtured Harmony became widely known in the West as the Summer Palace.

香山静宜园之琉璃塔

北京，1871年，50×40.5厘米

琉璃塔建于乾隆四十五年（1780年），是为迎接六世班禅而建。是一座亭塔复合体建筑，塔底部分为八面张开如伞的亭，塔身由琉璃砌成，塔刹为黄色琉璃宝瓶，塔中部悬挂铜铃56个。1860年，塔底八面伞亭遭英法联军焚毁，塔身躲过浩劫。

Glazed Tile Pagoda at the Grand Zongjing Monastery, Fragrant Hill

Beijing，1871，50×40.5 cm

This octagonal pagoda of seven storeys is 40 metres (130 feet) tall, and stands on an octagonal stone base. It was first completed in the mid-18th century, as a part of the Fragrant Hill project – one of another great construction projects Qianlong had embarked on. The Grand Zongjing Monastery was built to accommodate the sixth Panchen Lama during his stay in Beijing between 1778 and 1780. Although the monastery was burned down by French and British troops in 1860, the pagoda miraculously survived.

香山碧云寺石牌楼和金刚宝座塔

北京，1871-1872年，50×41厘米

碧云寺自元代创建，金刚宝座塔位于全寺最高点，建于乾隆十三年(1748年)，塔仿北京五塔寺形状建造，塔均用汉白玉砌造，是乾隆时期石雕工程的精品。前面汉白玉石牌坊，为四柱三间三楼二影壁，全坊雕琢精美，两侧连着石屏壁，壁上浮雕人物像，各像均有题名。所雕人物均为历史上"忠、孝、节、廉"的代表。屏壁左右再连石壁，亦有精美浮雕，如八仙过海等。

The White Marble Archway and Vajra Thorne Pagoda, Temple of Azure Clouds, Fragrant Hill

Beijing，1871–72，50×41 cm

Both the Archway and Pagoda were erected at immense cost in 1748. The magnificent Vajrasana Pagoda, which bears a striking resemblance to Bodhgaya Temple in India, is reached by a steep climb to a fine stone and marble three-arch gate topped with dragons. The pagoda, at 34.7 metres high, is the tallest of its type among China's existing pagodas. At the base of the pagoda is a high platform made of stone slabs with steps leading up to the top. There is also an interior passage to the roof with its group of square and flask-shaped stupas (small pagodas). Some are topped with metal umbrellas and all are lined with an astonishing collection of carved Buddhist images, including statues of Buddha, bodhisattvas, heavenly kings, guardians, dragons, phoenixes, lions, elephants and other animals and plants. In the grounds surrounding the pagoda is an amazing nine-branched Cypress tree.

十三陵长陵祾恩殿

北京，1871-1872年，50×41厘米

祾恩殿在长陵第二进院落内，即享殿，是祭陵时行祭典礼的大殿，明嘉靖年始定此名，意谓感恩受福。殿面阔九间，进深五间，黄瓦红墙重檐庑殿顶，坐落在绕以汉白玉护栏的高约3米的三层石台基上。祾恩殿由32根楠木巨柱支撑，最大的直径1.17米、高14.3米，如此整材楠木柱，世所罕见。

The Great Sacrifice Hall, Changling, the Ming Tombs

Beijing, 1871–72, 50×41 cm

Changling, the tomb of the Yongle Emperor, is the most magnificent Ming tomb in Beijing. Completed around 1413, it was one of a number of the Yongle emperor's grand projects. The Great Sacrifice Hall is situated in the second or sacrificial quadrangle, where imperial offerings were made to the emperor of a former dynasty. It is perhaps the most unique and impressive building within the complex. It has 32 pillars built entirely with teak from Yunnan. The ceiling is colourfully painted, while the outer roof of the Hall is covered in yellow glazed tiles.

十三陵神道上的石像生

北京，1871-1872年，50.5×41厘米

北京十三陵千米神道两旁，放置的石雕人、兽，古称石像生。共24只石兽和12个石人，造型生动，雕刻精细，深为来这里的摄影师所喜爱。其数量之多，形体之大，雕琢之精，保存之好，是我国古代陵园中罕见的。画面中的骆驼和大象，表示忠实善良，并能负重远行。在皇陵中设置这种石像生，主要起装饰点缀作用，以象征皇帝生前的仪威，表示皇帝死后在阴间也拥有文武百官及各种牲畜可供驱使，仍可主宰一切。

Stone Animals along the Approaches to the Ming Tombs

Beijing，1871–72，50.5×41 cm

Changling is approached first through an avenue protected by animals carved from limestone. Each species comprises two pairs, a kneeling pair and a standing one. There are 24 species, ranging from lions and unicorns to camels, elephants and 'qilin' (one of the four divine animals). All wear expressions of tranquil repose, 'thoroughly in keeping with their duty as the guardians of the dead'.

南口关沟

北京，1871-1872年，106×85厘米

关沟是今昌平区南口到八达岭之间的20公里长的峡谷。左侧是太行山余脉，人们称之为西山，右侧为燕山。关沟是两条山脉的分界沟。在地质构造上，这里是一个大断层。作为北京北方的门户，这里自古就是兵家的必争之地。汤姆逊特地让一人一驴入画，为肃杀的画面增添了一些人文意蕴。

Nankou Pass

Beijing, 1871–72, 106×85 cm

Nankou Pass, or the southern entry, is situated in Changping county in the suburb of Beijing. Sandwiched between two high mountains, it has been of strategic importance throughout history. From here one can see the first spur of the Great Wall. The Pass is very rocky and rough, and for centuries donkeys were the beasts of burden traders used for transporting goods through and beyond the Pass.

居庸关云台古门洞

北京，1871-1872年，153×111厘米

居庸关云台位于居庸关的中心，是元代大型过街喇嘛塔的基座，云台取其"远望如在云端"之意。创建于元至正二至五年（1342-1345年），是用汉白玉筑成的，上小下大，平面呈矩形。云台上原建有三座白色喇嘛塔，可惜毁于元末明初。台基中央门道可通行人、车、马，是当时南口重镇的一个交通要道。

Ancient Buddhist Arch at Juyong Guan, Nankou Pass

Beijing, 1871–72, 153×111 cm

The Ancient Buddhist Arch at Juyong Guan is situated at the most important section of Nankou Pass. It was here that the Mongols first entered north China in the 13th century. This marble Arch was built between 1342 and 1345 during the Yuan dynasty under the Mongols and decorated with carved figures taken from Indian mythologies.

居庸关云台古门洞石刻

北京，1871-1872年，51×40厘米

居庸关云台是元代一座大型的石雕艺术精品。券门内两侧壁及顶部遍刻佛像，佛像造型生动，雕刻技艺高超。六种文字的石刻经文、咒语为历史研究提供了难能可贵的资料。拍摄云台古门洞外景的摄影师很多，但像汤姆逊这样拍摄石刻细节的却凤毛麟角。

Interior of the Buddhist Arch at Juyong Guan, Nankou Pass

Beijing, 1871–72, 51 × 40 cm

The interior of this arch is elaborately sculptured with mythical Indian Buddhist figures – two kings of the Deva. The upper surface is covered with a multitude of small images of Buddha carved in bas-relief. Between the two Deva Kings is an inscription in Sanskrit with translations in Tibetan, Mongol, Manchu, Uyghur and Chinese.

八达岭长城远眺

北京，1871-1872年，50×41厘米

长城是中国古代劳动人民创造的奇迹。汤姆逊说，如果他的照片里没有一张长城的照片，也许这些照片是没有价值的。关于长城的照片，任何文字说明可能都是多余的。他还说，这张长城的照片不仅证明了他远足的范围，而且也说明他五年的行进不是一无所获。

View of the Great Wall at Badaling

Beijing，1871–72，50×41 cm

According to Thomson, 'no illustrated work on China would be worthy of its name if it did not contain a picture of some portion of the Great Wall'. For him, the Great Wall was an expression of a 'national characteristic of the Chinese race', for the Chinese, their country was the centre of the world. This photograph was taken at Badaling near the Nankou Pass.

仁慈堂废墟内景

天津，1871年，144×111厘米

天津仁慈堂是法国传教士在1862年所建的收容中国孤儿的慈善机构。1870年6月，慈善堂收容的中国儿童因发生瘟疫大批死亡，慈善堂将之葬于河东盐坨之地，每二、三人一棺，尸骸暴露，惨不忍睹，引起群众愤恨，慈善堂遭群众焚毁，堂中的十位修女被杀死，此事件和烧毁望海楼教堂一起，史称"天津教案"。这是慈善堂烧毁不久后拍摄的。

Interior Ruins of the Chapel of the Sisters of Charity

Tianjin, 1871, 144×111 cm

The Sisters first arrived in Tianjin in 1862 to perform charitable works. In 1870 in response to a cholera epidemic nearby, they received into the convent many sick children. A large number of these children died there, and due to a shortage of coffins, two or three were frequently buried together. This caused public outcry in the city. On 21 June, angry Chinese burned down many foreign mission stations, and massacred 21 foreigners in Tianjin, including ten nuns of the Sisters of Charity. The incident became known as the Tianjin Massacre. This photograph was taken not long after the event.

望海楼教堂废墟外景

天津，1871年，40×40.5厘米

法国天主教徒于1869年6月在天津租界外三岔口处修建，也叫天主教大会堂或胜利圣母堂，具有哥特风格。1870年，“天津教案”中内部被焚毁。图中教堂残存的木料正在被盗拆。1897年，望海楼天主教堂在原址上重建，1900年在义和团运动中又被焚毁。现存的建筑是1903年再次重建、1976年地震后又加以修复的。望海楼教堂几乎是天津近代史的标志性建筑。

Exteriors of Notre Dame des Victoires Cathedral

Tianjin, 1871, 40×40.5 cm

Notre Dame des Victoires Cathedral, also known as Our Lady of Victory Church or Wang Hailou Church, is a Gothic Revival building that stands on the right bank of the River Hai in Tianjin. First built in 1869, it was ‘the only striking object in the city’, according to Thomson, and a ‘dreadful eyesore to the natives, towering as it did high above any of their most sacred buildings, and drawing down evil influences from the sky’. The cathedral was destroyed in 1870 during the Tianjin Massacre and was not restored until 1896. The photo was taken in the year following the Massacre.

束发妇女

上海，1869年，48×40厘米

这位上海女子吸引汤姆逊的是她时髦的头饰。黑色的天鹅绒发网，带白色和浅蓝的花边，把女子乌黑的发辫隐藏起来，它的简洁让人过目难忘。天鹅绒在当时是进口奢侈品，在上海被认为是很时髦的饰品。中国妇女头饰是汤姆逊一个很重要的拍摄对象。

A Shanghainese Woman Wearing a Snood

Shanghai，1869，48×40 cm

This half-length portrait shows a woman wearing a black velvet snood with her hair encased. According to Thomson this way of wearing hair was very fashionable among women in Shanghai at the time. For him this simple style was 'quaint' and 'remarkable', yet he was perhaps unaware of its symbolic value for fashionable Shanghainese. Velvet was a relatively modern fabric, one probably first brought into China from Central Asia. In the second half of the 19th century it was regarded as a foreign luxury. During the time of Thomson's visit, Shanghai was beginning to emerge as a modern cosmopolitan city. A large number of its population, mostly migrants from nearby regions, aspired to everything foreign, which was a synonym for 'modern' and 'superior'. It was not surprising that this simple-looking snood was in vogue in Shanghai.

明孝陵神道石人

江苏南京，1872年，50 × 40.5厘米

坐落在古都南京钟山南麓的孝陵是明太祖朱元璋的陵墓，也是中国古代最大的帝王陵之一。长达1800米的神道上有四对身着盔甲或蟒袍的文臣武将，他们体型巨大，是明代石刻的艺术珍品，拍摄时石人保存还相对完好。汤姆逊在说明中写到：这些宏伟的武士表情平静、仁慈，似乎对他们守卫死人的工作很满足。有趣的是，石人下两位中国人模仿石人相视而立，两相对比使人们知道了石人的巨大体积，这两人极有可能是汤姆逊雇佣搬运器材的中国“苦力”。

Ming Tomb

Nanjing, Jiangsu，1872，50 × 40.5 cm

The tomb of Zhu Yuanzhang, the first Ming emperor, was for Thomson one of the few traces of Nanjing's former glory. Situated on the Zhongshan hill near to the city's eastern wall, it was one of the largest mausoleums in imperial China. What seemed to impress Thomson most was the giant stone statues of warriors guarding this splendid monument: 'the calm, majestic repose and benign expression of these stone warriors, who seem pleased with the task of guarding the ashes of the dead'. The two natives in the picture were most likely coolies that Thomson had hired to carry his photographic equipment. Their presence a ccentuate the enormous size of the stone warriors.

金陵机器制造局

江苏南京，1872年，50×41厘米

由李鸿章倡导的金陵机器制造局诞生于1865年，是晚清洋务运动中开办较早、规模较大的兵工厂之一，其主要产品有枪、炮、弹药、火药、水雷等。汤姆逊在游记中充分肯定了工厂先进的管理方式，同时也对工厂是否会改变购买劣质原材料和雇佣廉价劳动力的传统做法而深深忧虑。

Nanjing Arsenal

Nanjing, Jiangsu, 1872, 50×41 cm

Nanjing Arsenal was built in 1865 under the auspices of Li Hongzhang, the renowned Late Qing general and statesman, who negotiated with western powers on several occasions on behalf of the Qing government, and who advocated modernizing the Chinese army. The Arsenal was one of the first of its kind in China, and, under the superintendence of Sir H. Macartney, was run on the most up-to-date scientific principles. Every year some hundred tons of guns and ammunition were manufactured here, from heavy guns for battery trains to field artillery, howitzers, gatling-guns, torpedoes, rockets, shot, shell, cartridges and caps.

汤姆逊在金陵制造局

江苏南京，1872年，40.5×43.5厘米

这张照片取景和前一张基本相同，不同的是照片里的人，他们不再是工厂里的工人，而是约翰逊自己跪在地上，好像在进行武器测试，这也是汤姆逊中国之行中仅有的几张有自己影像的照片。旁边的两个站立者也不再是上一照片的工人和官员，很可能汤姆逊雇佣的中国“苦力”。

Nanjing Arsenal

Nanjing, Jiangsu，1872，40.5×43.5 cm

This was one of the very few photographs Thomson took in China in which he appears himself. Here he was trying out newly manufactured field artillery. While Thomson remarked on the Chinese ability to produce weapons, he was also deeply worried about the poor quality raw material and the underpaid labourers used at such places.

重建工地

江苏南京，1869-1870年，111.5×119厘米

1853年，太平军攻入南京，并确定为自己的都城，改名为天京。11年后的1864年，清军和外国军队收复并洗劫了南京。当汤姆逊几年后到达南京时，很多“被毁坏的街道空无一人”。不过，城市重建已经开始了。这张照片表现的就是一群苦力正在一所寺庙旁劳作，监工是身穿长袍的一个和尚。

Reconstructing the City of Nanjing

Nanjing, Jiangsu, 1869–70, 111.5×119 cm

In 1853 Taiping rebels captured the ancient 'southern capital' Nanjing and made it its 'Heavenly Capital'. Some ten years later, in 1864, the Qing and foreign troops crushed the Taiping's Heavenly Kingdom and sacked Nanjing. When Thomson visited Nanjing a few years later, the city had literally become 'many dreary acres of demolished streets with not a single occupant'. Yet he noted that an active restoration had just begun. The photo shows a group of coolies at work near a temple, while a Buddhist priest wearing a robe supervises them.

天后宫

浙江宁波，1870-1871年，50×40.5厘米

天后，民间俗称妈祖，是中国沿海百姓崇拜的海神。宁波天后宫，又名庆安会馆，始建于宋代，清代重修。它既是祭祀天后妈祖的殿堂，又是行业聚会的场所，占地面积约5000平方米，系我国八大天后宫和七大会馆之一。也是一座集砖雕、石雕、朱金木雕等宁波民间工艺于一体的传统建筑精华。

Ningbo Tianhou Temple or Qingan Guildhall

Ningbo, Zhejiang, 1870–71, 50×40.5 cm

Ningbo Tianhou temple was a late Qing reconstruction of the Song period Tianhou temple. The reconstruction took place in 1850 with donations from overseas Chinese shipping merchants; thus parts of the complex also functioned as a guildhall for those merchants. Because the original temple was built by a native of Fujian, and Tianhou was a Fujianese goddess, the temple was also referred to as the Fujian temple. After the reconstruction it was renamed Qingan Guildhall, meaning to celebrate the goddess for pacifying the raging sea. This reconstructed temple is the most magnificent building in Ningbo, and according to Thomson, it was the finest example of temple architecture in China. Huiguan or Guildhall was an important institution during the Ming and Qing periods, a place where people from the same profession or region could meet. In the imperial capital, Beijing, some of the guildhalls also provided accommodation for those who had travelled to the capital to take imperial examinations.

天主教堂遗迹

江西九江，1872年，40×41厘米

江西九江上通重庆，下达上海，是一个名副其实通江达海的内陆港口城市。九江港在鸦片战争后被清政府列为通商口岸，从此赣北门户洞开。照片中的拍摄地距离九江十英里，据说是当时中国最大的一个天主教堂，教堂是被太平军焚毁的。汤姆逊通过遗迹里的巨石雕刻推断，教堂可能和1596年来到这里的意大利籍传教士利玛窦有关。站立的中国老妪更增加了这里的苍凉气氛。

A Religious Ruin

Jiujiang, Jiangxi, 1872, 40 × 41 cm

According to Thomson, this photograph was taken in a small town called Taiping kung, about ten miles from Jiujiang. The area was close to Bailu Cave in Mount Lu, where the observed neo-Confucian scholar Zhu Xi once stayed. Although Thomson was told this was once a famous Buddhist monastery, he observed the ruin resembled the pointed Gothic apertures of a medieval European building. He thought at one point that it might be a Jesuit mission. However, Matteo Ricci only stayed in the Nanchang area, and there is no record of him building a mission near Mount Lu. The old lady in the photo is there perhaps to accentuate the antiquity of the ruin.

方广岩寺僧人

福建福州，1870-1871年，40.5 × 48厘米

福州方广岩寺（即汤姆逊记述的“永福寺”）是建在半山腰的一座小型悬空寺。寺里只有三名僧人。照片中的两位僧人，坐着的老者是位盲人，右侧这位身强体壮。照片中未出现的还有位僧人是个孩子。汤姆逊和他的“苦力”曾经在这里夜宿。

Two Buddhist Priests at Fang-guang-yan Monastery

Fuzhou, Fujian，1870–71，40.5 × 48 cm

Fang-guang-yan monastery was located 30 miles from Fuzhou on the upper reach of the Min River. It was for Thomson the most interesting of all the sites near Fuzhou. During his visit he befriended the three monks dwelling there. The old priest shown in this photograph was blind and, according to Thomson, quite infirm. The younger one however was an 'able bodied, good natured youth'. Each day they strictly kept their ritual observances, as recorded here.

方广岩寺吃饭的僧侣

福建福州，1870-1871年，42.5×40.5厘米

方广岩寺的三个僧侣中，包括右侧的一个年轻活泼的孩子和中间瘦弱的盲眼老者。他们通常只吃蔬菜，每个人都吸烟，其中的老人很可能还抽鸦片。福建气候炎热潮湿，很多人吸鸦片来预防疟疾和减轻病痛。

Monks Eating at Fang-guang-yan Monastery

Fuzhou, Fujian，1870–71，42.5 × 40.5 cm

Here Fang-guang-yan's three monks are at the meal table. The youngest one was a boy 'full of vivacity'. According to Thomson their diet comprised only vegetables. However, he noted that all three of them were smokers and liked to indulge in tobacco. Thomson also suspected that the older man smoked opium. Fujian, being a sub-tropical region, harboured a variety of tropical diseases, including malaria. Before the advent of modern medicine, local people regularly used opium and tobacco as a prophylactic against malaria and as relief for miasmic fever.

方广岩寺里敲钟人

福建福州，1870-1871年，40.5×42厘米

方广岩寺虽然不大，但还是给汤姆逊留下了深刻印象。三位僧人每天恪守规制，晚上太阳落山时，他们便身着黄色法衣去庙里念经；而每天早上，这位强壮的和尚就会定时敲响庙里的大钟，他们便又开始一天有规律的寺庙生活。

A Monk Ringing the Bell at Fang-guang-yan Monastery

Fuzhou, Fujian，1870–71，40.5×42 cm

Thomson's trip to Fang-guang-yan monastery is sometimes regarded as the most artistically accomplished of all his photographic journeys. Situated at the summit of a high mountain, the monastery is almost as difficult to reach as it is to enter the 'Heavenly door'. In addition to the location Thomson was deeply impressed by the monastery's architecture: 'It looks like nothing I have ever seen or dreamed of seeing, with its broad eaves, carved roofs and ornamented railing painted in the brightest hues'. Of his stay there, he recalled that each morning he was awoken by the monks chanting or by the ringing of the bell as seen here.

鼓山涌泉寺

福建福州，1870-1871年，41×40.5厘米

福州市鼓山涌泉寺为"闽刹之冠"，寺建在海拔455米的鼓山山腰，创建于唐代。涌泉寺当时也是很多当地外国人夏天避暑的场所。这张照片从高处俯视，充分表现出处于山林中涌泉寺的美丽、宁静与超然。

Yongquan Monastery, Drum Mountain

Fuzhou, Fujian, 1870–71, 41×40.5 cm

In the second half of the 19th century, Yongquan monastery was a favourite place of resort for both foreigners and Chinese in the hot summer months. It is said to have taken its name, Yongquan, or the 'Bubbling Spring', from a spring of clear cold water in its vicinity. The monastery comprises a number of detached buildings set one behind the other in a spacious paved courtyard. This photograph was taken from the hill just above the monastery and shows the tranquility and beauty of the place.

鼓山涌泉寺僧众

福建福州，1870-1871年，40.5×48厘米

被誉为"闽刹之冠"的涌泉寺在最盛时，僧人曾达1500多人，汤姆逊到达时这里有200多僧人。他对这些僧侣的长袍十分感兴趣，认为风格很像古代欧洲人的服饰。照片中僧人们一身素衫，神态悠然。

Buddhist Priests at Yongquan Monastery, Drum Mountain

Fuzhou, Fujian, 1870–71, 40.5 × 48 cm

Yongquan monastery is situated seven miles from Fuzhou, halfway up Drum Mountain. It was thought to have been built in the 9th century and then rebuilt several times during the Ming and Qing. One of the most magnificent religious buildings in Fujian, it was an important centre for studying Mahayana Buddhism. At the time of Thomson's visit, about 200 monks lived there. He was intrigued by their robes, which he thought resembled closely the monastic garb of medieval Europe. He even came to believe that Buddhism and Roman Catholicism shared certain similarities.

金山寺

福建福州，1870-1871年，52×40.5厘米

金山寺位于福州西郊洪塘村附近乌龙江上。建于宋代，是福州唯一的水中寺。金山寺原是江心的小石阜，因为它的形状像石印浮于水面，有如江南镇江之金山，故曰"小金山"。主要建筑物有观音阁、大悲楼、金山塔等。现在的金山寺系1934年重建的，因限于地形，寺院没有巍峨的殿阁和巨大的佛像，但玲珑精巧的建筑倒映在水中，分外别致。

Jinshan Temple, River Min

Fuzhou, Fujian，1870–71，52×40.5 cm

Jinshan Temple, or the 'Pagoda Anchorage', as Thomson called it, is situated on the River Min, just west of Fuzhou. It is the only temple in Fujian that sits on the water. Due to the location, its style of construction is rather simple, with the result that not many visitors have been impressed by it. Thomson perhaps inspired by Taoist and Buddhist landscape art,deliberately created a space so that the island appears to exist in isolation. This and the stillness of the water contribute to the effect of near-perfect serenity.

外国人居住区

福建福州，1870年，102×85厘米

1842年中英《南京条约》签订后，福州是第一批被迫开放的五个通商口岸之一，也是中国的主要茶叶市场之一，大批外国淘金者蜂拥而至，一座座小洋楼拔地而起，里面有俱乐部、图书馆和网球场。汤姆逊到达福州时，福州的外国居住区已经具有相当规模。

Foreign Settlement

Fuzhou, Fujian，1870，102×85 cm

Although Fuzhou was one of five ports made open to foreign residents by the Treaty of Nanjing in 1842, another decade passed before the city finally entered into trade with foreign countries. Its chief export was tea, and in 1863 over 50 million pounds of it were exported from Fuzhou. Money brought a flood of foreign traders to the city, and a great number of foreign missionaries were also active in the area. By the time of Thomson's visit, Fuzhou's foreign settlement was well established, boasting an excellent club, library and racket court. The settlement is built on the south bank of the River Min, separated from the main city by a bridge and a small island. It has a mixture of Chinese and European-style houses.

殖民地风格建筑

福建福州，1870-1871年，48×40.5厘米

汤姆逊到达福州时，这里的外国社区已经成熟。可以看出这座西洋风格的建筑周围绿树成荫，风景如画。照片中几个外国人似乎很享受这里的风景。

A Colonial-Style House

Fuzhou, Fujian, 1870–71, 48×40.5 cm

By the time of Thomson's visit Fuzhou had a well-established foreign settlement, which was 'picturesquely situated on eminences which command extensive views of the country around . . . Many varieties of European flowers and vegetables are grown here to great perfection by the Chinese gardeners. It is altogether a sort of place where foreigners may well be content to reside'.

轿子

福建，1870-1871年，42×40.5厘米

轿子是中国古代一种特殊的交通工具，大致有两种形制或类型，一种是不上帷子的凉轿，也叫亮轿或显轿；一种是上帷子的暖轿，又称暗轿。不同的官品，在轿夫的数量、轿子的形制类型、帷子的用料颜色等方面都有严格的区分，处处显示着封建社会里森严的等级制度。从照片看，这是一种四人抬的凉轿。

A Sedan Chair

Fujian, 1870–71, 42 × 40.5 cm

Until the advent of modern vehicles, the sedan chair was one of the main means of carriage in China. Mandarin officials and people of wealth and rank kept their own private sedans. Mandarin officials in particular, indicated their rank by means of marks on the frame and cover of their sedans, and by the number of bearers and footmen in attendance. Sedan chairs could also be hired, just as taxis are today.

教堂

福建福州，1870-1871年，49×40.5厘米

从19世纪中期开始，大批传教士就来到了福州。除了用中文和地方话传教外，一些医学传教士也投入了反对鸦片的活动，希望借此得到地方官员对传教的支持。大部分传教士建立了自己的教堂。这个石头教堂由英国传教士于1850年建造，位于闽江南岸不远的山上，它的对面是一所中国人的庙宇。

A Church

Fuzhou, Fujian，1870–71，49 × 40.5 cm

Missionaries began to be active in Fuzhou in the mid-19th century. Apart from producing and distributing tracts and parts of the Bible prepared in both Chinese and the local dialect, a number of medical missionaries were also actively involved in the anti-opium movement, hoping to gain support for their missionary work from the local gentry. Most missions in Fuzhou set up their own churches. This stone-built one was constructed by the Anglican Church of England. It was built in 1850 on the hill near the southern bank of River Min. Close to the church there was also a Methodist chapel and a Christian cemetery. Opposite it, however, was a Chinese shrine. According to Thomson, devout Buddhists regularly burnt incense there to counteract the influences of the Christian places of worship.

万寿桥上的人群

福建福州，1870-1871年，40×42厘米

福州万寿桥，现叫解放大桥，为闽江上最古老的一座石桥，已有600多年的历史了，如果从它的前身浮桥算起，就有近900年了。这座用巨大的花岗岩建造的石桥，除了石栏杆外并没有过多的装饰，但方便和实用也许是建造者最初的设想，历经千年，巨大的桥石完好如初。古朴的石桥吸引了汤姆逊，而桥上的人群则成为了照相机的焦点。

View of Wanshou Bridge

Fuzhou, Fujian，1870–71，40×42 cm

Wanshou Bridge, formerly called the bridge of 'Ten Thousand Ages', was thought to have first been built in the 9th century. Its present-day name, 'Bridge of Liberation', hardly conveys its historical significance. About one quarter of a mile long Sand thirteen or fourteen feet wide, it was built in stone. At the time of Thomson's visit it was used solely by pedestrians and for transporting goods. Here we see a large crowd standing on the bridge, probably made up of curious locals watching Thomson taking his photograph. But Thomson perhaps was trying to show the ingenuity of ancient China, whose people were able to build such a colossal structure, one that brought great convenience to local life.

万寿桥全景

福建福州，1870-1871年，40×42厘米

这张照片展示了万寿桥的巨大。当时的万寿桥全长391米，宽4.5米，桥下有36孔水道。每孔之间叠架两根1米见方，长9米，重逾40吨的大石梁，上面再用厚20-30厘米的石板横铺。当时石桥上还有商铺，后来为了行人和交通都被移开了。

Long View of Wanshou Bridge

Fuzhou, Fujian, 1870–71, 40×42 cm

This photograph shows the immense size of the bridge. It has nearly forty solid stone buttresses. Some of the stones are almost 3 feet square, and 45 feet in length, extending from buttress to buttress, acting as sleepers. Above these stone sleepers lie a granite platform. There are strong stone railings on the sides of the bridge, which are fastened to stone pillars. Originally there were shops on this bridge, but they were later removed to make way for passengers and transport.

挑水的农妇

福建福州，1871年，40.5×42厘米

在福州郊区，很多山坡荒地被开垦成了梯田，一年能种三茬庄稼。这些福州的妇女每天挑水来浇灌自己的农田，以使土地更加肥沃。汤姆逊在描绘这些农妇时说：她们很强壮、健康和有吸引力，褐色的脸颊熠熠闪光，光滑的黑发用银饰或鲜花装饰。她们衣着朴素，但很干净，她们不裹脚，但脚上精美的绣花鞋还是吸引了人们的目光。

A native Woman Carrying Buckets

Fuzhou, Fujian, 1871, 40.5×42 cm

This photograph was taken near to a tea plantation on terraced hills just outside of Fuzhou. Terraced fields were common in the Fujian countryside. To fertilize them the native women had to transport human manure from the city of Fuzhou. They did not bind their feet, and they carried the same burdens as the men did. Hard work rendered these women strong and healthy. According to Thomson, 'their olive cheeks are warmed with a glow of colour'.

采茶的妇女和孩子

福建福州，1871年，40.5×42厘米

福州当时是中国主要的茶叶生产和出口地，周围乡村里布满了茶园。汤姆逊参观了福州北部15英里外的一所茶园。通常茶园都是穷苦人从地主手里租来的，规模都不大，租户种茶，最后按协议价格把茶卖给土地主人。这些妇女和孩子都是雇来采茶的。

Women and Children from a Tea Plantation

Fuzhou, Fujian，1871，40.5×42 cm

Fuzhou was the main centre for tea production and export, its countryside is dotted with tea plantations. Thomson visited one plantation in terraced hills about 15 miles north of Fuzhou. There the farms were usually small, seldom exceeding a few acres in size, and were rented by the poor from landlords, who paid the land tax. The tenants undertook to dispose their crops to the landowners at a certain stipulated price. The fields were able to yield three crops each year, and many locals grew tea for the simple reason that it was the most valued cash crop. Thousands of poor women and children like these shown here were employed to pick out stems and stalks from the crop.

茶园里的妇女

福建福州，1870-1871年，40.5×41厘米

这群妇女是当地的一个茶园雇佣的，在汤姆逊的眼中，这些福建妇女强壮、健康、很有魅力。她们光滑的黑发上用各种银饰和鲜花装饰，她们的服饰款式简单，但干干净净，她们也不裹脚，但她们天生的小脚配上美丽的绣花鞋还是很吸引人的。

Native Women from Fujian at a Tea Plantation

Fuzhou, Fujian, 1870–71, 40.5×41 cm

This group of women were employed by a local tea plantation to work on the farms. According to Thomson they were strong and healthy, and many of them he thought were attractive to the eye: 'their glossy black hair is decked with silver ornaments and fresh flowers. Their dress is simple and remarkable for its bright cleanliness. They never bound their feet, but rather draw the eye to their natural smallness by wearing prettily embroidered shoes'.

铜匠铺

福建福州，1870-1871年，40.5×42厘米

在中国之行中，汤姆逊对中国工匠的精湛技艺印象深刻，很多手工艺人在他们破旧的门店里制作出了一个个奇迹。汤姆逊评价这些工匠是令人尊敬和不可缺少的人。在这个福州铜匠铺里，铜匠“能够充分利用金属的延展性，从一个扁片打造成形状各异的物品”。铜匠精湛的技艺估计也使现场的几个本地人着迷了，他们都目不转睛地欣赏着。

A Chinese Coppersmith at Work in His Shop

Fuzhou, Fujian，1870–71，40.5×42 cm

Throughout his journeys in China, Thomson was always impressed by the ingenious feats of workmanship he encountered, and the fact that so many craftsmen could produce wonders in front of their humble doorways. He praised the artisan as highly respectable and indispensable, ‘never ashamed of his craft or the music that rings from his anvil’. One such is this coppersmith he visited in Fuzhou, who was able to ‘take full advantage of the ductility of the metal . . . by beating it from flat sheets into the most varied and complex forms’.

白鹿洞

福建厦门，1870-1871年，51×40厘米

白鹿洞位于虎溪岩背后。明朝始建寺，清乾隆年间重修，增建三宝殿、朝天洞、六合洞等。三宝殿后有宛在洞，洞中伏着一双泥塑白鹿，口向石罅。夏季炎热时，罅中常有烟雾涌出，缕缕可见，故称“白鹿含烟”，为厦门小八景之一。现在所存景观为1993年重建，并开放给游客游览。

White Deer Grotto

Xiamen, Fujian, 1870–71, 51 × 40 cm

Situated on the Yueping Hill in Xiamen, White Deer Grotto was thought to have once accommodated the celebrated Neo-Confucian scholar Zhu Xi, and from him derived the name, for Zhu Xi was intimately connected to the famous White Deer Academy in Jiangxi. Just as White Deer Academy had been established as a place for scholarly retreat, White Deer Grotto has long been a favourite place for summer retreat. According to Thomson, from the Grotto one enjoyed a commanding view of Xiamen.

南普陀寺

福建厦门，1870-1871年，40×51厘米

南普陀寺位于厦门市区五老峰下，是厦门著名古刹。建于明代永乐年间(1403-1424年)，明末（1628年）毁于兵火。清康熙二十三年（1684年），靖海侯施琅将军重建，因寺院以侍奉观音菩萨为主，又位于我国四大佛教道场之一的浙江舟山普陀山之南，故称南普陀寺。

Southern Putuo Monastery

Xiamen, Fujian, 1870–71, 40×51 cm

Southern Putuo Monastery is one of the most important Buddhist sanctuaries in Fujian. It was first built in the early 15th century, though its history may be traced back to the Tang (618–907). Because it is dedicated to Guanyin, as is the monastery at Putuo Mountain in Zhejiang, it was therefore given the name Southern Putuo Monastery. Over the years the monastery has expanded into a massive complex, and in modern times it has become one of the most important Buddhist teaching institutions in China.

日光岩

福建厦门，1871年，42×40.5厘米

日光岩俗称“晃岩”，位于厦门鼓浪屿中部偏南的龙头山顶端，为鼓浪屿最高峰。岩顶筑有圆台，站立峰巅，凭栏远眺，厦门风光尽收眼底。岩石上还有许多书法石刻，记录着这里的历史。

Riguang Rock

Xiamen, Fujian，1871，42×40.5 cm

The hills by the harbour of Xiamen, on the island of Gulangyu, are crowned with a series of conspicuous rocks. The most prominent one, known as Riguang Rock or 'Sunshine Rock', allegedly was given its name by a local hero, the anti-Qing Zheng Chenggong. The rock is engraved with text passages connected with the area's history. Many people believed the rocks were closely linked to local Feng-shui, so they revered them greatly, trusting the rocks would bring good fortune to the port.

育婴堂

福建厦门，1870-1871年，43.5×41厘米

19世纪，由于战乱和贫穷，厦门杀害女婴的现象非常普遍。当地一个商人建立了一所育婴堂来收容那些人们不想要的孩子。当地人通常以极便宜的价格把孩子卖给育婴堂，女孩5便士，男孩3英镑。想领养孩子的人可以来到这里免费认领一个。

A Foundling Hospital

Xiamen, Fujian ，1870–71，43.5×41 cm

In the 19th century, as result of extreme poverty and war, female infanticide was particularly high in Amoy. A local merchant set up a foundling hospital to care for unwanted children. Often the locals sold their girls to the hospital for as little as five pence, whereas a boy might fetch as much as three pounds. Anyone wishing to adopt a child could go to the hospital and be given one free of charge, provided he could show he was perfectly respectable.

商店

福建厦门，1870-1871年，41×40厘米

汤姆逊被中国的商店深深吸引了，从香港到北京，他拍摄了大量商店的照片。这张照片是两位老人在厦门的一家粮店里。从1842年《南京条约》签订后，厦门作为第一批通商口岸，贸易额不断增长，这里首要的商品是茶、糖和粮食。茶和糖主要是出口，而大量的大米是从台湾和泰国买进的。

A Chinese Shop

Xiamen, Fujian, 1870–71, 41×40 cm

Thomson was fascinated by China's shops. From Hong Kong to Beijing, he took many photos of various types. This one shows two old men inside a grain shop. Since the treaty of Nanjing in 1842, the trade in Amoy had grown considerably. The chief commodities in the area included tea, sugar and grain. Tea and sugar were grown mainly for export, while large amounts of rice were imported from Formosa (Taiwan) and from Thailand.

民居

福建厦门，1870-1871年，50.5×40.5厘米

20世纪后，很多人觉得厦门是一个浪漫的海滨城市，但在汤姆逊到达厦门时，除了外国人或当地富商在远离市区的山顶或鼓浪屿岛上建造了些漂亮的房屋外，市区的房屋不但拥挤，还破败不堪。布满鹅卵石的小巷里，狭长、阴暗、凹凸不平，从这张图片中可见一斑。

Residential Quarter

Xiamen, Fujian，1870–71，50.5×40.5 cm

Although many people today regard Xiamen as a romantic coastal city, in the second half of the 19th century it was seriously dilapidated. Other than a few handsome houses that belonged to wealthy merchants and Europeans, situated either on the top of the hill away from the city or on the island of Gulangyu, the houses in the city itself were crowded together. Many of them were in a terrible state of decay and the long, dark and narrow streets paved with cobblestones were so worn and loose that 'they rest for the most part in treacherous pits of mud . . . if a foot be placed hastily on the rocking flag, a shower of most offensive dirt is splashed up over one's clothes'.

汤姆逊和两个清兵

福建厦门，1871年，120×111厘米

厦门是第一次鸦片战争后清朝首批开放的通商口岸之一，汤姆逊来到之时已有大量西方人在此生活。这张照片是汤姆逊在中国旅途中拍摄的为数不多的自己的肖像。从照片的构图来看，不知是汤姆逊想拍摄个人的肖像，还是想拍摄和这两个清兵的合影。当时没有自拍装置，应当是汤姆逊的翻译或"苦力"帮助他完成拍摄的。

Thomson with Two Manchu Soldiers

Xiamen, Fujian，1871，120×111 cm

Amoy, or Xiamen, was the southern frontier of the Qing empire. Although the Manchu finally managed to conquer the region, it continued to cause great difficulties to imperial rulers. In 1729 the Qing court introduced its first anti-opium edict to the area, as a means of social control. Although in 1842 the Qing government was forced to grant the British the right to trade freely in Amoy, it continued to station its army there. In its attempt to suppress the local branch of Taping rebels, the Qing army was reported to have brutally slaughtered a great number of the natives. In this photograph, Thomson appears together with two Manchu soldiers. Possibly he was trying to show that the city had fallen into the hands of outsiders: the Manchu and the Europeans.

夫妻

福建厦门，1870-1871年，85×105厘米

这是身穿传统服饰的一对厦门夫妻。根据中国习俗，当时的夫妻是不会有这样对望的姿势的，这肯定是沟通大师汤姆逊的杰作。虽然他们的表情有点勉强，目光也没有完全相对。

An Amoy Couple

Xiamen, Fujian，1870–71，85 × 105 cm

Although this couple are sitting closely together, the husband looks away. In traditional China it was improper for a couple to face one another. It seems that the scene was set up by Thomson, but the couple look rather hesitant.

夫妻站立肖像

福建厦门，1870-1871年，120×112厘米

这是同一夫妇一张站立在欧式房屋前的全身照。汤姆逊是为了展示他们的服饰和总体形象。根据服饰来判断，这对夫妇家境相对较好，就像另一张照片两人对望一样，男子的叉腰姿势也突破了中国人双手下垂的传统站姿，使画面增添了些许生动。

An Amoy Couple

Xiamen, Fujian， 1870–71， 120 × 112 cm

This is a full-length portrait of the same Amoy couple that stand in front of a European-style house. Thomson's intention was to show the costume and general appearance of local people. This couple are dressed well, in particular the woman with her beautifully embroidered silk robe. This suggests they were from a fairly wealthy family. According to Thomson there were quite a few wealthy Chinese merchants living in Amoy at the time, living in beautiful, upmarket houses.

闲谈的妇人

福建厦门，1871年，42×41厘米

汤姆逊是偶然碰见这两名妇人的，当时她们正在站着闲谈，汤姆逊建议她们坐下，会比较放松。当时右侧年龄大一点的妇人正在讲述一个医生用黑色的膏药给她医治头疼的经历。而左侧的妇人是一个保姆，她在讲述如何在主人家逃避额外的家务劳动和震慑顽皮小孩子的心得。照片中人物表情真实、自然，体现出了拍摄者对普通人的理解和同情。

Two Amoy Women Gossiping

Xiamen, Fujian, 1871, 42×41 cm

Gossip is universal, and for Thomson the women of Amoy were of no exception. In this photograph, however, he does not stereotype his subjects, but treats them as individuals: the older one wearing a patch on her temple enjoying the tittle-tattle of daily life; and the seemingly friendly nurse who might in reality be somewhat cunning and duplicitous.

三个厦门人

福建厦门，1871年，42×41厘米

画面当中是个男子，两边是女人。三个人眼神都看着下方，好像不舒服的样子。这两个女人也出现在另外一幅坐着说话的照片中，是汤姆逊建议她们坐下拍摄的，那样会显得更放松和自然。而这幅照片中的三人都没有说话，很可能是汤姆逊想表现中国传统男女授受不亲的状况。

Three Amoy Natives

Xiamen, Fujian, 1871, 42×41 cm

Here are two women with one man standing in the middle. All three look down, as if they are uncomfortable. The two women appear in another photograph, seated and gossiping. It was Thomson's suggestion that they sit down to have the photo taken, so that they would look more relaxed and natural. That photo does not include the man, for Thomson wanted to record the women chatting at their ease. In this photo, however, both the women are silent while the man does the talking.

劳力

福建厦门，1871年，40.5×41.5厘米

照片中两个人的相貌和服饰是厦门劳力的典型代表。一个肩扛稻草，一个手提食篮。汤姆逊描述说，厦门的劳力是非常贫苦的，一个壮丁每天挣5便士，而一个技术工也不过挣8便士。艰苦的生活迫使很多人去海外当劳工，中国劳工在美国和东南亚国家得到了很高的评价。

Two Field Labourers in Amoy

Xiamen，1871，40.5×41.5 cm

Here two field labourers pose for the camera, one carrying straw on his shoulder, the other with a food basket. According to Thomson, the people in the Amoy area were quite poor: an able-bodied man earned five pence a day, while skilled workmen were only paid about eight pence. The hard life forced many to seek work abroad, for Chinese labourers were highly rated in America and Southeast Asian countries.

苦力

福建厦门，1870-1871年，40.5×41.5厘米

这些人是厦门当地的普通苦力。虽然满清已经统治厦门多年，但他们依旧保持了自己的传统，说当地的语言，维持原有的服装风格，他们把满清强加给他们的辫子塞到了头巾里。在那个时期，就有很多人到美国或南洋打工。

Amoy Natives

Xiamen, Fujian, 1870–71, 40.5×41.5cm

Within the Qing empire, Amoy men were known to be rebels or 'southern rascals', who frequently caused problems for the authorities. Although the Manchu had finally conquered the region, many local people continued to maintain a separate identity. Not only did they speak a different dialect, they dressed in a unique style. Here two men wear turbans, which hide the queues (pailted hair) imposed on them by the Manchu. According to Thomson, both men were local coolies. At this time many such men left to work in America or in plantations in Southeast Asia.

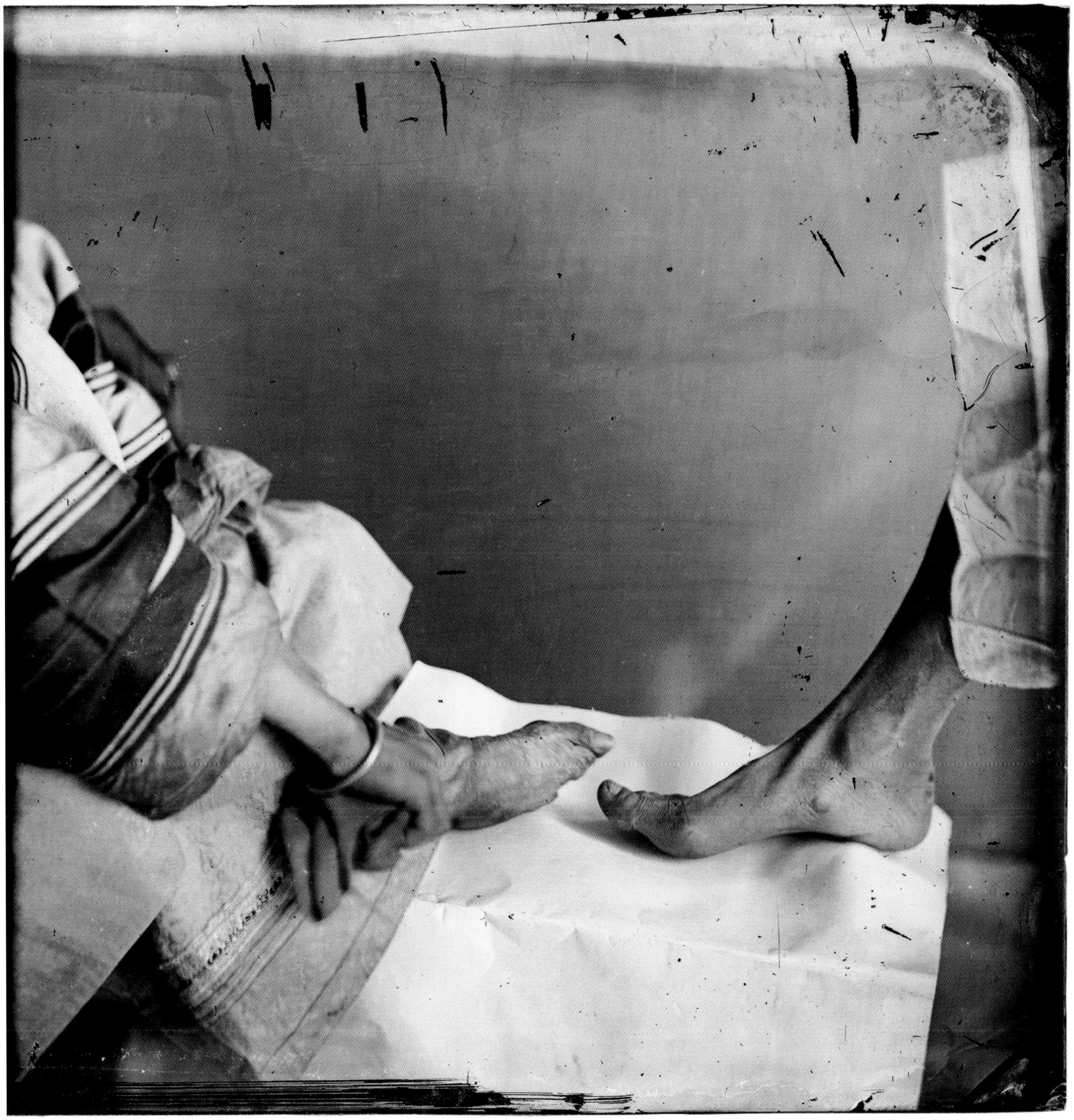

女人的裹脚和天足

福建厦门，1871年，40.5×41厘米

中国妇女的裹脚是外国人很感兴趣的一个现象，尤其对摄影师来讲。汤姆逊说：中国人告诉他，不可能纯粹通过给钱来让女人解开裹脚拍摄的。最后，汤姆逊是在厦门一个很开明的中国人的帮助下，才得以在一个私下的场合拍摄了这张照片。但无论汤姆逊怎样努力，也说不动这位妇女再把衣服掀高一些来拍摄她畸形的踝骨了。

The Bound and Unbound Feet of Two Amoy Women

Xiamen, Fujian，1871，40.5×41 cm

The bound feet of Chinese women have always fascinated Westerners. Time and again during his travels in China Thomson had tried to get a woman to let him photograph her bound feet, but he failed to do so until he reached Amoy. This photograph contrasts a bound foot against a natural foot. According to Thomson, he had to pay both women handsomely to get the shot. It shows there was a price for art, even in the 19th century.

妇人

福建，1871年，40.5×43厘米

这是福州附近一个当地妇女的半身侧面肖像。她坐在凳子上，耳朵上戴着大耳环，头上被银饰和鲜花装点。常年的户外劳作和日晒使她的皮肤看起来很黑，就像汤姆逊所说：黄褐色的皮肤闪着温暖的光亮。

A Native Woman

Fujian，1871，40.5×43 cm

This is a half-length profile portrait of a native woman from the hills near the city of Fuzhou. Seated, she wears large earrings and a coiffure with elaborate silver decorations and fresh flowers. Sun and hard work outdoors have rendered her skin quite dark, or as Thomson described it, olive in colour with a warm glow.

贞节牌坊

福建，1870-1871年，42×41厘米

在古代，牌坊是一种表彰性的建筑，贞节牌坊这一事物起源于宋代。为了表彰遵循封建礼教的妇女，就以国家的名义，对守节不改嫁、且能孝敬公婆、悉心抚育幼儿的妇女树立贞节牌坊。在明清两代最为盛行。今天，这些贞节牌坊已成为封建社会荼毒妇女的见证。

A Pailou Dedicated to a Virtuous Widow

Fujian，1870–71，42×41 cm

A pailou is an ornamental memorial arch set up in memory of the noble deeds or virtues of the deceased. In imperial China it could only be erected with special permission from the emperor. In general, if a wealthy man had done something remarkable, he might during his lifetime erect a pailou for himself at his own expense. A virtuous widow, however, who had reached the age of 50 without remarrying might be permitted to erect an arch to commemorate her life, and the imperial treasury would allow her a small sum to do so. This type of pailou can commonly be seen in rural China, in particularly the area between Fujian, Zhejiang and Jianxi. The practice is thought to have begun in the 11th century with the emergence of neo-Confucianism. According to Cheng Yi (1033–1107), a renowned Neo-Confucian scholar, it was better for a widow to starve to death than to remarry.

闽江夕照

福建，1870-1871年，50.5×40.5厘米

闽江是福建省最大的河流。汤姆逊在福建时被闽江的美丽深深吸引了。这张照片在闽江口所拍摄，远处为五虎山。应当是夕阳西下时逆光拍摄，极具美感和浪漫情调。

River Min

Fujian, 1870–71, 50.5×40.5 cm

During his visit to Fujian, Thomson was captivated by the beauty of River Min. Responding to the magnificent landscape, he developed a sensitive aesthetic style, fine yet sharp. This photograph was taken against the bold mountains in the background. These are the Wuhu or 'Five Tiger' Mountains, and it is here that the river widens into a basin with narrow openings at either end. The photo seems to have been taken at sunset, which adds a romantic tone to the image.

官员

广东广州，1869年，111.5 × 149厘米

这是汤姆逊作为一个肖像摄影师的代表作品。虽然这位官员直视镜头，姿势也是平常中国人习惯的坐姿，但他一侧脸部是有阴影的，这种在西方很流行的明暗对比的技法在当时是不被中国人所接受的。根据汤姆逊的记录，他是一名六品文官。

A Cantonese Mandarin Official

Guangzhou, Guangdong, 1869, 111.5 × 149 cm

This is a fine example of Thomson's work as portrait photographer. The subject looks directly at the camera, the pose in which all 'men of taste' in China would like to be photographed. However, there is a shadow hiding half of the man's face, a chiaroscuro art technique unacceptable for portraiture in China at the time. According to Thomson this man was a sixth-grade mandarin official and a man of letters who possessed two degrees in imperial examinations. He is dressed in official costume, which corresponds to his rank. Although his salary from the government might be small, with bribery and extortion he could earn up to ten or even 100 times the amount of his official pay.

两广总督瑞麟

广东广州，1869-1871年，40.5×50.5厘米

瑞麟，字澄泉，叶赫那拉氏，满洲正蓝旗人。历官道光、咸丰、同治三朝，人称“瑞中堂”。他1864年上任广州将军，1865年开始担任两广总督。汤姆逊写道：也许两广总督是欧洲人最熟悉的中国官员，由于近离香港，瑞麟和很多欧洲官员都有不错的私交。汤姆逊拍摄的中国官员很多都着便装，表情轻松，可能摄影者更多地想从一个平常人的角度来发现他们的喜怒哀乐。

Ruilin, the Governor of Guangdong and Guangxi

Guangzhou, Guangdong, 1869–71, 40.5×50.5 cm

For Europeans, Ruilin was one of the better-known Chinese officials of the late 19th century. Born a Manchu, Ruilin entered public service at an early age but only rose to high government position at the age of 45. In 1865 he was appointed the governor general of Guangdong and Guangxi, where he dealt extensively with the British. He was often praised for his perfect courtesy and for his genuine intention to cultivate a friendly relationship with the British. Under his administration Guangdong prospered, and there was a greater degree of public contentedness there than had been known for many years.

华林寺住持

广东广州，1869-1870年，66×41厘米

华林寺是广州佛教四大丛林之一，距今已有1400多年，历隋、唐、宋、元、明诸代，传灯不绝。1849年，该寺住持抵园和尚奉诏始建总面积为1364平方米的五百罗汉堂，除供奉三宝佛外，还陈列着神态各异的泥塑五百罗汉像，成为当时外国摄影师镜头的焦点。但汤姆逊却把镜头对准了这里住持的私人庭院，他介绍，这位华林寺的住持大半生时间都隐居在这里，他很喜欢养花，其中有一株盛开的睡莲。

The Abbot at the Temple of Five Hundred Gods

Guangzhou, Guangdong, 1869–70, 66×41 cm

This is the private courtyard at the 'Temple of Five Hundred Gods' or the 'Magnificent Forest Temple' in Guangzhou. Situated in the western suburbs of the city, it was thought to have been founded by Bodhidharama, a 6th-century Buddhist missionary from India. As a guest of an official of the local Customs office, Thomson was well received at the Temple and shown to the Abbot's private quarters. This courtyard, according to Thomson, was adorned with a variety of rare and beautiful flowers, including a splendid specimen of the Sacred Lotus. The Abbot was devoted to the plants and pleased to share his fondness for flowers with his foreign guest.

老妪

广东广州，1868-1870年，40.5×53厘米

汤姆逊虽然是在大街上拍摄的这位老妪，但照片很像一个照相馆的作品。关于这位老妪和他的丈夫，汤姆逊在照片说明中写道：他们的儿子和孙子已经支撑起了这个家庭，但这位老妪仍然忙着家务。她针线活很熟练，在别人病倒时是个很好的护士。她的头发已经变细和发白了，但她每天都精心地梳理和呵护它。汤姆逊独特的拍摄视角，和老妪独特的姿势产生了巨大的视觉冲击力。

An Old Cantonese Woman

Guangzhou, Guangdong, 1868–70, 40.5 × 53 cm

This is perhaps one of most interesting photographs Thomson took during his travels. It can be regarded as a street photograph, but it is at the same time a beautiful formal portrait. It shows his talent as a street photographer, yet he brings to his art the skills of studio photography. Here Thomson wanted to show all the hardship and toil the old woman had endured, and also her resilience: 'Her hair has grown thin and white, but she still dresses it with neatness and care'; she 'still busies herself in the lighter domestic duties; she is skilful with the needle, and invaluable as a nurse in time of sickness'.

富家小姐

广东广州，1869-1870年，107×111厘米

肖像是汤姆逊中国之行拍摄的一个很重要的内容。为了更多展现不同人的生活侧面，汤姆逊拍摄了大量不同的中国人肖像，尤其是女人的肖像。这位女子站在走廊尽头的门口，她的服饰和时髦的头饰提示着我们她来自富裕之家，而左手手扶门框的姿势对传统中国人拍摄的直立姿势来说也是一个突破。

A Cantonese Woman

Guangzhou, Guangdong, 1869–70, 107 × 111 cm

Portraits were a vital aspect of Thomson's photographic work and a regular source of his income. Throughout his photographic journeys in China, portraiture remained a key feature. While adapting to the native taste for picturing the subject straight on, Thomson also tried to give as accurate a record of a wide range of Chinese society and life as possible. Among different groups of people, he was particularly interested in portraying women of varied social backgrounds, from affluent Cantonese ladies to their maids, to ordinary peasant women in Fujian, to Manchu brides. This Cantonese lady is wearing a silk robe and a stylish hair ornament. The backdrop is an elaborately carved doorway on a verandah. Her costume and background suggest she is from a well-to-do family.

两个年轻女人

广东广州，1869-1870年，40×41厘米

照片中的两个女人穿着同样的丝绸服装，站在房屋走廊外的木栅栏边，左边的妇女还手持一朵鲜花。当时广州是中国丝绸的生产和贸易中心，而丝绸衣服是富裕人家的妇女最喜欢的衣料，同时也是一种社会地位的标志。对汤姆逊来说，选取此景寓意着她们的生活“也像篱笆一样被禁锢着”。

Two Young Cantonese Women

Guangzhou, Guangdong，1869–70，40 × 41 cm

Both these women standing by a wooden fence outside the verandah of a house wear identical quilted silk costumes. The one on the left holds a flower. Their hair is also wreathed with flowers and their faces had been painted 'until they resembled their native porcelain ware'. For Thomson these were signs that suggested their lives were 'hedged round with so many restrictions'.

贵妇

广东广州，1869-1871年，111×151厘米

汤姆逊在说明中详细描述了这位贵妇人化妆的过程：她首先用热的湿毛巾擦脸，然后把一个圆盘里的脂粉放到一个化妆盒里，轻轻地按压脂粉，小心地涂抹在脸颊上，这样光滑白皙的皮肤上出现了淡淡的红色。右手精美的折扇和左手长长的指甲套也透露出她的社会地位。贵妇神情安详、淡定，一派大家闺秀风范。

A Cantonese Beauty

Guangzhou, Guangdong, 1869–71, 111×151 cm

This young woman wears a fine silk robe, holds an open painted fan and stands before a folding screen painted in Chinese themes. Both the fan and screen are more in the chinoiserie style. It is known that a large number of these types of 'Chinese things' had been produced in the Pearl River Delta area since the 18th century exclusively for the European market. It is interesting to note that this woman has a slight 'non-Chinese' look about her. As noted by Thomson, some of the Chinese he encountered in this part of China had pale skins, finely formed features and large lustrous eyes, which suggested they might not be of 'purely Chinese blood'.

老者和孩童

广东广州，1869-1871年，40.5×49厘米

典型的中国式照相构图，典型的广式家具（太师椅和方几）。长者的威严和孩子的顺从跃然纸上。但两者都没有什么表情，这种僵硬的模式和汤姆逊的肖像风格格格不入，他更喜欢把人拍摄得生动有趣，这可能是不得已而为之的情况。

An Old Cantonese Man and a Young Boy

Guangzhou, Guangdong，1869–71，40.5 × 49 cm

This photograph shows Thomson often had to conform to the established rules of Chinese portraiture. The sitter is posed in the centre, facing the camera, with a child on one side and a tea-table on the other. On top of the table sits a teacup. The face of the old man and the boy remain expressionless: in the Chinese tradition, the photo is a record of the person rather than that of the personality. This rigid style was quite contrary to Thomson's own portraiture style, with latter the subject often appearing more human and vivid, and the backdrop more interesting.

商人和助手

广东广州，1869-1871年，112×140厘米

清末广东商人是一个独立的阶层，在大清政府和西洋贸易中充当着一个重要的角色。他们平常以炫耀其豪华私宅及陈列的昂贵制品——比如丝绸、象牙、珠宝、瓷器和绘画等来进行彼此间的竞争。当然在照相时也不示弱，身着当时只有王宫贵族才穿的貂皮大衣。

Three Chinese Merchants

Guangzhou, Guangdong，1869–71，112 × 140 cm

This is another of Thomson's formal Chinese-style portraiture. The two older men are seated in front while the younger one stands behind. All three men looked square on at the camera. This arrangement of sitters reflected the hierarchy within traditional Chinese society. The man on the left wears a fur coat. Fur was a fashionable luxury in 19th-century China and thus a sign of wealth, and therefore greatly desired by the rising professional class in coastal towns, including the compradore, which is who this sitter is. The rise of the compradore was a peculiar feature connected to mercantile life in Chinese open ports in the second half of the 19th century and into the 20th century. The compradore swere native Chinese employed by foreign companies to run businesses locally. Although a number of compradores had become economically well off and fairly successful in business, their social position was never recognised, and until recently they were given very little credit in China.

女仆

广东广州，1869-1871年，41×40.5厘米

　　她身为仆人，但衣着整洁，发髻梳理得一丝不苟，佩戴耳环，两个手腕上还带着玉镯，只是淡淡忧伤的眼神透露出她对命运的无声抗争。

A Cantonese Lady

Guangzhou, Guangdong，1869–71，41×40.5 cm

This portrait was taken in an artist's studio. The simple backdrop includes a table covered with embroidered Chinese cloth; on the side are examples of European-style furniture and two candlesticks. The young woman was probably an artist model, or a customer who was having her portrait painted when Thomson visited the studio.

学童

广东广州，1869-1870年，85 × 104厘米

汤姆逊对中国孩子的学习能力深为赞赏，他说中国的孩子在学习中完全可以和欧洲孩子并驾齐驱。他还对中国当时的教育产业的某些进步给予肯定，比如政府资助在部分学校开设外语和科学课程，在福州船政学堂，学生可以学习航海、建筑、工程和机械等课程。

A Cantonese Schoolboy

Guangzhou, Guangdong, 1869–70, 85 × 104 cm

Although Thomson often quibbled about the old system of education in China, he was greatly impressed by the diligence and aptitude of Chinese schoolboys, and their capacity in acquiring knowledge. He also noted in different parts of the country there were attempts to modernize the education system, and some schools had adopted western learning. This boy is wearing a queue (plaited hair) and holding a board and a book in his hands. He looks straight ahead rigorously, as if he is looking into the future.

船妇

广东广州，1869-1870年，40.5×48.5厘米

广州很多贫困家庭吃住在他们赖以生存的小船上，小船不仅是他们的家，也是他们的收入来源，一般一家人都会住在船上。虽然贫困，但照片中船妇的衣服很干净，头发梳理得一丝不乱。两位船妇的相向而视，是汤姆逊为了突出她们的黑发和健康的褐色皮肤，这一点是汤姆逊觉得很有吸引力的地方。

Two Cantonese Boat Women

Guangzhou, Guangdong, 1869–70, 40.5×48.5 cm

Until the 1950s, a great number of people in Guangzhou, also in Hong Kong, lived on boats. For the poor, boats provided a more comfortable way of living and also a source of regular income. Boat people also enjoyed a greater degree of freedom, using the boat as their means of transportation. Often a boat was occupied by an entire family. This photograph shows an old woman and a younger one facing each other. The intention was to highlight the glossy black hair and the olive skins of working-class Chinese women, which Thomson found particularly attractive.

船家女

广东广州，1869-1870年，111×124厘米

当时船家没有结婚的女孩都要在自家的货船上帮助装卸货物，她头上的格子方巾是为了遮挡阳光。像她这样的贫苦女子，在结婚前一般都是把头发编成辫子盘在头上，前面可以留少许刘海。虽然穿戴朴素，但女孩眼神里还是透露出掩饰不住的青春和妩媚，这样的女子表情在早期中国肖像作品中十分罕见。

A Boatwoman

Guangzhou, Guangdong，1869–70，111 × 124 cm

This portrait has a very modern appeal. Unlike the majority of portraits made in the 19th century, the backdrop here is particularly plain, setting off the simple headscarf and costume the woman is wearing. The sparkle in her eyes shows she is completely at ease. During his visit to Guangzhou and Hong Kong, Thomson had encountered a number of boatwomen, and was greatly attracted by their natural beauty. They never used makeup and always dressed simply; they were the prettiest and most attractive-looking women he had came across in southern China.

身穿蓑衣的船夫

广东广州，1869-1871年，40.5×41厘米

大清年间广州船夫的生活是贫苦的。传统中国文学中"一蓑一笠一扁舟"诗句透露出更多的是名士在逍遥中却又深藏着几许萧瑟、孤寂的情感。但汤姆逊抓取的这位身着蓑衣、头戴斗笠的船夫，更突出的是他健美的身姿和温情的眼神。

A Cantonese Boatman

Guangzhou, Guangdong，1869–71，40.5×41 cm

According to Thomson, the boating population in southern China was extremely poor and miserable: 'Millions of these hardy sons of toil live from hand to mouth, and are only kept from starving, from piracy, and from rebellion by the cheapness of their staple food, and by the constant demand for their labour'. It was thought because of their simple diet they had to resort to alcohol to keep themselves warm in the winter. Whenever they had a spare scrap of cash they spent it on drinks. This boatman standing against a wall wears a brimmed hat, a woven cape and a jerkin with tufted hems. Although posed, with his legs crossed at the ankles, he looks fairly relaxed.

新郎和新娘

广东广州，1869-1870年，40.5×50厘米

中国封建社会几千年的爱情婚姻史就是一部"父母之命，媒妁之言"的历史。汤姆逊在照片描述中写道：他们没有求爱的过程，结婚日期是算命先生来决定的。当把新娘从父亲那里接上新郎轿子后，他们就在小乐队的伴奏下，穿过熙熙攘攘的街道来到新郎家。从照片看，一对新人脸上没有丝毫的幸福，两人分别注视不同的方向，连高明的沟通大师约翰逊也无可奈何了。

A Cantonese Bride and Groom

Guangzhou, Guangdong, 1869–70, 40.5×50 cm

In this photograph Thomson wanted to show China's strange marriage customs – the arranged loveless marriage, the red-coloured wedding dress, as against the white bridal dresses to be seen in Europe; and the power imbalance between the groom and his future wife. This groom is dressed in a mandarin robe and looks rather sullen. The bride wears a veil and cap, and for Thomson this was a sign that she was deprived of her privilege of having a glimpse of her future husband. This wedding portrait contrasts hugely to those made in the same period in Europe.

旗人清兵

广东广州，1869-1870年，52.5×40.5厘米

汤姆逊写道：当时在广州有1800名旗人，但他们不能按时发放津贴，所以大部分人很贫穷，并且逐渐丧失了他们民族的骠悍特性。这群旗人士兵是英国驻广州领事的中国卫兵，拍摄于广州领事的花园内，背景中的古塔就是六榕寺花塔。汤姆逊拍摄时并没有让他们全副武装、手持兵器，而选择了一种休闲的状态，却带给我们更多的回味。

A Group of Manchu Soldiers

Guangzhou ,Guangdong，1869–70，52.5×40.5 cm

These Manchu soldiers were guards for Sir D. B. Robertson, the British consul at Guangzhou at the time of Thomson's visit. According to Thomson there were 1,800 Manchu soldiers in Guangzhou at the time, forming part of the government's permanent garrison. Many of them, although extremely poor, were physically strong and fit, and so 'they would still make good soldiers'. A number, including these men, were in fact trained in the system of European drill and the use of foreign arms.

满族清兵

广东广州，1869-1871年，33×40.5厘米

这位清兵应当是英国驻广州领事的中国卫兵之一。虽然他们的境遇在广州1800名旗人当中应当是好的，但从照片中已经看不出当年八旗兵的勇猛和彪悍，也许是广州浓厚的商业氛围，更加衬托出这些只会习武的旗人的没落吧。但这样的姿势使人看着很放松，体现了汤姆逊的摄影风格。

A Manchu Soldier

Guangzhou, Guangdong, 1869–71, 33 × 40.5 cm

This portrait is more Thomson's style. The soldier appears completely at ease with his right arm resting on the wall. He looks away from the camera, with the hint of a smile on his face. The photograph is obviously posed, but it reveals the essence of humanity. It also shows the 'fine manly build and soldierly appearance' of the typical Manchu soldier.

街头赌博

广州，1868-1871年，40.5×51厘米

汤姆逊在提到中国的赌博时说：在赌博过程中，你可以看到中国人在寻求刺激时的性格特点。这里没有充满热情的惊呼，没有令人冲动的嘈杂，没有极度喜悦的释放，也没有对命运深深的诅咒。在这里，你只能从赌博人的脸上看出一点激动的迹象，或是一脸愠怒、铁定心肠去冒险的心态。直到幸运之神又向他们微笑，或是离他们而去，使他们沦为乞丐。

Street Gamblers

Guangzhou, Guangdong，1868–71，40.5 × 51 cm

Gambling was prevalent in 19th-century China. Although this photograph was obviously posed, it captures the true atmosphere of street gambling and the character of a gambler: the vitality and the menace. Thomson focused particularly on the face of the standing gambler. According to him, only in the faces of Chinese gamblers can one 'see the signs of emotion, or the sullen determination to carry on at all hazards'.

街头赌博

广东广州，1869-1871年，111×148厘米

清末，赌风在中国盛行。由于清政府的禁赌令，使很多人开始转入地下活动，从此带来更多的腐败和犯罪。这张照片表现的是街头"苦力"路边赌博的场景，从几个人表情来看，少的是赌博的功利色彩，更多的是一种休闲放松。

Street Gamblers

Guangzhou, Guangdong, 1869–71, 111 × 148 cm

In the late 19th century gambling was a popular vice throughout southern China. Government legislation banning it did not contain the problem on the contrary it forced gamblers to go underground, and the result was an increase in corruption and crime. Gambling was not confined to gambling houses, for it also took place in clubs and private homes. For the poor labouring class, streets were a common gambling venue.

盲艺人

广东广州，1869-1871年，85×93厘米

两位艺人手持的是南方的琵琶和台湾的竖琴，被约翰逊称为东方的吉他和小提琴。但这些艺人当时并不为人所尊重，主要为民间婚、丧、喜、庆时所雇请。除了固定的演奏曲目，他们有时还根据时事或当地生活即兴演奏一些曲目。

Two Blind Cantonese Musicians

Guangzhou, Guangdong，1869–71，85 × 93 cm

As Thomson observed, wandering minstrels were a Chinese institution. In most cases the musician was blind, but would be accompanied by a sing-song girl, who tuned his lute and sang simple ballads to his music. The instruments shown here are now known as the 'southern lute' and 'Taiwan harp'. Both instruments were originally from Central Asia. Since the 19th century, they have been present in popular local singing performances throughout southern China, especially in Guangdong and Hong Kong. Such performances were seen in a wide range of venues, from brothels to homes of the elite, and they were always performed by blind musicians. In addition to traditional themes, musicians often provided improvisations on current affairs and local life. These two musicians were hired for festival celebrations.

珠江风景

广东广州，1869-1870年，50×40厘米

珠江是中国南方最大河系，中国七大江河之一。原指广州到入海口的一段河道，后来逐渐成为西江、北江、东江和珠江三角洲诸河的总称。当时的广州依靠珠江，一年四季都可以接纳来往的大货轮，广州与本省其它地区的来往都是通过珠江的几条支流，以及遍布该地区的小运河和水道漕运。一条汽船航线，还将广州和香港连接起来。

View of Pearl River

Guangzhou, Guangdong，1869–70，50 × 40 cm

Covering an area of 200,000 square miles, with three branches, Thomson described the Pearl River as the most interesting watercourse in China along with the Yellow River and Yangtze. The Pearl River delta was extremely fertile and still is one of the most important agricultural regions in China. At the time of Thomson's visit he noted that every inch of soil was used to grow rice, sugar, tobacco, mulberry, fruits and vegetables. This photograph shows the vastness of the river. In the background stands a pagoda, confirming for Thomson that in this part of China pagodas were in fact watch-towers, for they always commanded an extensive view of the surrounding landscape. The man sitting by the river brings life to the scene, the addition of a human figure being one of the techniques Thomson used regularly in his landscape images.

商船

广东广州，1869-1871年，86 × 39.5厘米

图中行驶的商用帆船由广东建造，是当时南中国最快的船只之一，看似笨重，但行驶起来可抵御一般的风暴。这些商船的拥有者都是一些小的贸易商，有的船员也有股份。

A Junk

Guangzhou, Guangdong, 1869–71, 86 × 39.5 cm

'Junk' is a European term for a Chinese sailing vessel. The term comes from the Javanese word jong, meaning large vessel. According to Thomson the vessel shown here 'is a fine type of its class, and has in her model something of the foreign ship, though retaining quite enough of the old Chinese build to soothe the prejudices of the nation.' In the 19th century this type of junk was usually popular with traders, and they were often 'well-armed, carrying . . . half-a-dozen smoothbore guns of foreign make for six or eight-pound shot, a number of matchlocks, and a quantity of ammunition'. This image is a quintessential late-19th-century visual representation of the South China Sea; similar ones can be seen in a number of western drawings of the same period.

古之楚庭牌坊

广东广州，1871年，40.5×48厘米

位于广州的"古之楚庭"石牌坊初建于1644年，1867年重建。该坊为两柱一间一楼的花岗岩牌坊，石柱上刻有"同治六年次丁卯孟春吉旦众善信捐资重建"。柱断面呈方形，下有基石，与前后抱鼓石同置于一大石板上。坊额下为小额坊。两端各由一石雕花雀承托。枋下部略呈月梁之状。额板东西面分别篆刻'粤秀奇峰"、"古之楚庭"。"楚庭" 是人们当时所知的广州最早使用的名字，牌坊现位于越秀公园越秀山中山纪念碑下。

Ancient Chuting Stone Memorial Arch, Yuexiu Mountain

Guangzhou, Guangdong, 1871, 40.5×48 cm

Situated in today's Yuexiu Park near the top of Yuexiu Mountain, this stone memorial arch was first erected in 1644 and then rebuilt in 1867 with the money donated by a group of Buddhist believers. The location was thought to be the historical site of Chuting, the ancient name for Guangzhou. Hence the arch was named the 'Ancient Chuting Stone Memorial Arch'. This photograph was taken from the east side; the inscription reads 'Yuexiu, the Magnificent Summit'. On the staircase leading up to the arch are three beggars. As Thomson observed, in the late 19th century in major Chinese cities there was often 'a motley crowd of beggars' loitering outside religious buildings.

苦力

广东汕头，1871年，40×42.5厘米

聚焦、关注底层的社会是汤姆逊在中国拍摄时的一个特点。平常很多人并不关注的情景在汤姆逊的镜头中活灵活现起来。七个苦力服饰、姿态各不相同，裸露的肌肤以坚硬的山岩作为背景，凸显出了人性的坚韧。

Chinese Coolies

Shantou, Guangdong, 1871, 40 × 42.5 cm

In the mid-19th century, each year a large number of labourers from Shantou and nearby regions left their homes to work on plantations in Cochin China (Vietnam), Siam (Thailand) and the Straits of Malacca. Chinese labourers were much in demand in Southeast Asia because of their willingness to undertake the hardest work. For these economic migrants, the main attraction of working abroad was the pay. At two or three dollars a month, their earnings were much higher than what they could receive back home. After having saved enough money, many would return home to buy a plot of land.

汲水泵

广东汕头，1871年，40.5×42厘米

这张照片是在汕头附近的韩江所摄，韩江是广东省第二大河流。汤姆逊拍摄这张照片的时候正值旱季，水位太低，灌溉不易，必须靠这个木造的汲水泵人工来打水进行灌溉。

Irrigation on the Han River

Shantou, Guangdong, 1871, 40.5×42 cm

This is the left bank of the Han River near Shantou. During the dry season local people often employed chain pumps for irrigation. The pump normally consisted of a long square wooden tube into which an endless chain was fitted, carrying a series of wooden diaphragms separated from each other by about six inches. The diaphragms descended over guiding rods above the tube, and returned again at great speed to raise the water in a continuous flow. At its upper end the chain traversed a wheel having a series of spokes. The chain outside was made to rotate by pushing it down with the foot.

妇女

广东汕头，1871年，41×50厘米

这张照片中的妇女梳着当地特别的发髻。这位妇女隆鼻、削颊、短人中，牙齿白而整齐。汤姆逊说：当地妇女的发髻千变万化，值得西方人作为一个课题来研究。这可能也是汤姆逊拍摄大量中国妇女发髻的原因吧。

Female Coiffure of a Shantou Clan

Shantou, Guangdong，1871，41 × 50 cm

This photo shows a styles of female coiffure belonging to a clan in the Shantou region. In Chaozhou and Shantou, while the main population group are the Teochew, there are also other ethnic groups, such as the Hakka, Punti and others. Each group has its own dialect and distinct culture and customs, and throughout the 19th century, clan disputes were a regular recurrence in the region. In his portrayals of different types of female coiffures, Thomson occasionally adopted a certain racial stereotypes. For instance, he saw the female in this photo represented a 'facial type', which 'is one peculiar to certain of the natives of Swatow. The nose is prominent, well-formed, and straight, the upper lip short, the teeth white and regular, and the chin well cut'.

外国人居住区

广东汕头，1871年，48.5×40.5厘米

汕头在第二次鸦片战争后被迫成为通商口岸，早在开埠之前，已经有大量外国人在汕头非法聚居了。这是从理查森公司不远处的山上向下拍摄的。居住区已经有了大量的花园和草坪。周围一个中国人的小村落也正迅速发展，用以提供这些外国人生活所需。

A Foreign Settlement

Shantou, Guangdong, 1871, 48.5×40.5 cm

Shantou, situated on the eastern coast of Guangdong, is both densely populated and very fertile. In the second half of the 19th century its main attraction for foreign traders was its spacious harbour, which was deep enough for large vessels to anchor in. In 1858 it became an open port and a formal foreign settlement was built up four years later in an area known as Kakchio (Queshi, as it is called today). Because the settlement was situated on a hill comprising barren rocks, rich soil from the plain was imported so that the foreign residents could enjoy gardens and lawns. The houses of Europeans were built with native concrete and in colonial styles with verandas. The large one in the photo is said to have been the residence of Messrs. Richardson & Co., the boss of a sugar merchant company from Glasgow in Scotland. Besides being a port, Shantou and its surrounding area was also famous for its sugar production. In the mid-19th century Shantou alone exported about one million piculs (1 picul equals about 133 lbs.) of sugar annually.

凤凰塔

广东潮州，1869-1870年，48.5×40.5厘米

凤凰塔位于广东潮州古城外东南约2公里处的韩江之滨，因遥对凤凰山，又与隔江的凤凰台相望，故名。凤凰塔始建于明万历十三年（1585年），清乾隆三十年（1765年）重修。塔高45.8米，7层八面，砖石结构，近400年来，虽经台风、洪水、地震考验，仍昂然屹立。汤姆逊写到，虽然很多人认为这是佛塔，但这样的塔在越南和柬埔寨却很少见，因此，这种塔更应该是一座瞭望塔。

Phoenix Pagoda

Chaozhou, Guangdong, 1869–70, 48.5×40.5 cm

The physical remains of remote past civilizations have fascinated European travellers for centuries and Thomson was no exception. In southern China he came across a great many pagodas, and for him the Phoenix pagoda near Chaozhou was the best example of this type of architecture. Phoenix pagoda is a seven-storey stone building with exquisite carvings, each storey had an inner stone patterned flooring. This stone-built pagoda was first erected in 1585. The terraces are surrounded by massive stone railing resting on solid ornamental stone brackets, though many of the railings are damaged. In the 1918 earthquake the top two storeys were destroyed. Although, wrote Thomson, this type of pagoda is generally regarded as a Buddhist monument, they are rarely seen in Cambodia or Vietnam. Thus he believed they were in fact intended to serve as watch-towers.

乡村风景

广东，1870年，146×111厘米

这是汤姆逊在广东乡村一座小山上拍摄的风景。近处是中国特色庙宇，中间是平整的农田，远处山峦叠嶂，云雾蒙蒙，山脚下嫩绿的竹林在风中摇曳，就像一片翠绿大海里泛起的波浪。汤姆逊在说明中十分感慨，说从来没见到过这样美丽的耕田。

A Bamboo Grove on the Bank of North River

Guangdong, 1870, 146×111 cm

This photograph was taken during Thomson's trip on the North River, a branch of the Pearl River. He was completely struck by what he saw: 'The cultivation hereabouts was of a kind I had never seen before; in the foreground were a multitude of fields, banked off for the purposes of irrigation, but already shorn of their crops; here and there was a mound covered with temples and trees, and beyond, reaching to the base of the distant mountains, were groves of green bamboo, rocking their plumage to and fro in the wind, like the waves of an emerald sea'. This natural beauty inspired him to take the photograph to give his readers some idea of 'the grandeur of the inland scenery. The vast plain covered with graceful bamboo or the luxurious green of the paddy fields, contrast abruptly with the background '...

女童

广东，1869-1870年，111×147厘米

在汤姆逊的中国之行中，为孩子拍摄肖像是最困难的。因为很多中国人觉得外国人的照相机是很神秘和危险的设备，尤其对孩子们而言。在这张照片中，女孩表情自然，没有任何害怕的表情，从她的头饰和装束看，肯定是来自富裕的家庭。根据汤姆逊的描述，这个女孩的光彩很快将会泯灭，因为她不能上学，清秀的脸庞未来将会被厚厚的化妆所覆盖。

A Chinese Girl

Guangdong, 1869–70, 111 × 147 cm

Throughout his journeys in China, Thomson found that portraits of children were particularly difficult to obtain. This had to do with Chinese suspicion about foreigners and about the camera, regarding it as a mysterious and dangerous instrument of destruction. That children in particular should be shielded from. Nevertheless, as Thomson admitted, there were times when he was shown extreme kindness and openness by the locals. This portrait shows a little girl looking straight at the camera with no fear in her eyes. Her headdress and outfit suggest she was from a fairly well-off family. According to Thomson, however, her natural sparkle would soon be diminished: she would have no opportunity to attend school and her comely face would be covered with thick makeup. That was the fate of a Chinese girl in the 19th century.

贵妇的女仆人

广东，1869-1871年，42.5×40.5厘米

这个女仆是主人在她小时候从她父母那买过来的。在这张照片里，女仆是在她去市场采购的路上，其实她比她的女主人有更多外出的自由。她左手持一漆盒用来盛购买的蛋糕和糖果，右手持一巨大的扇子来遮蔽强烈的阳光，不知是为了保护自己的皮肤，还是为了保护盒里的糕点和糖果。

A Cantonese Maid

Guangdong, 1869–71, 42.5×40.5 cm

Ordinary individuals remained a central focus of Thomson's work. When portraying lower-class people Thomson attempted to show their human side, their true characters, their contradictions and often their charm. Here we have a maid on her way to market. According to Thomson her slave status in fact gave her more freedom than her mistress enjoyed. In her right hand she holds a huge fan to protect her from the sun. Here the fan is an object of fascination for Thomson, as it symbolized another 'Chinese contradiction': he reported that the Chinese generally dislike shadows on their faces when they have their photographs taken, 'yet all of them carry fans in order to secure that very shade so essential to existence in the south of China'. Here the maid's face is clearly marked by shadows, which add to her charm and beauty. It shows Thomson did not always bow to the Chinese portraiture tradition.

拿阳伞的贵妇

广东，1869-1871年，41×41厘米

这位广东贵妇吸引摄影师的应当是她的长柄阳伞和长长的发髻。伞是中国人的发明，这种长柄折叠伞一般是以竹为架，纱纸蒙顶，桐油漆，用来遮挡广东强烈的阳光。而贵妇的高髻都是用假发掺和衬垫梳理而成的，以簪或钗相固定，样式豪华，很吸引眼球。

A Chinese Lady Holding a Parasol

Guangdong, 1869–71, 41×41 cm

In China Thomson had a particular interest in women's hair. Although he found that Chinese hair was uniformly black and straight, there was great diversity of styles throughout China according to the prevailing local fashion. This image shows a lady with an elaborate hairstyle, which Thomson described as 'chignon par excellence'. The chignon was made by a professional hairdresser and wearing one meant that the woman had to sacrifice her comfort when sleeping. This photograph was taken at full length showing the woman holding a closed parasol. The parasol was another example of Thomson's proof that shade was essential to the life of southern Chinese.

飞来寺两位僧人

广东，1869-1871年，40.5×48厘米

飞来寺在清远县北江小三峡之飞来峡右岸，又名峡山寺。以佛教徒的墓地而闻名。汤姆逊说："和尚们隐居那里，远离尘世，他们认为什么时候能从宇宙万物中认识了抽象的自我，什么时候就会忘记存在，忘记喜怒哀乐，从而达到绝对的清静，进而修成正果——涅槃"。

Two Buddhist Priests

Guangdong，1869–71，40.5×48 cm

Thomson was not only fascinated by sacred structures and monuments, he also showed much interest in the lives of religious men. Typical of the Victorians he often catagorised his portrayals of people. For him there were basically two types of Buddhist priest in China, those of southern China and those of the north. These two men are Thomson's 'typical Buddhist priests of southern China': both men, with their heads shaven, are dressed in long robes with very wide sleeves. 'To keep a daily reckoning with Heaven', the older priest wears a rosary around his neck, while the younger man holds one in his hand. For Thomson the features of each of these priests were 'those expressive of weakness of character', thus 'no foreigner would care to trust him out of sight with a coin, far less with the future welfare of his soul'.

画师

香港，1869年，78×40.5厘米

在摄影术刚发明时，由于没有放大和彩色摄影技术，香港照相馆的画像业曾一度繁荣。画师主要根据照片来画，收费多少依据画幅大小来定，顾客大部分是当时来港的外国海员。学徒画手和脚，师傅画面部，流水作业，一般24小时完成画像和装框。该照片充分表现了画店的环境，是了解早期香港照相业的重要实证影像。

这张照片初看很像当时流行的一种立体照片。立体照片是用双镜头照相机拍摄而印制出的一种特殊的照片。人的两眼之间有距离，从两个不同的位置看物体，产生了视觉差，从而感受到了立体效果。立体相机就是根据这一原理而发明出来的。立体相机有两个镜头，镜头间的距离与人的两眼间的距离相同。两个镜头分别成像，拍摄出两张照片。这两张照片冲洗出来后，放在特制的观片器中观看。观片器上也有两个透镜，透镜间的距离也与人眼间的距离相同。所以通过观片器同时看两张照片，可以感受到一张前后景分离的立体照片的效果。

立体照片就像20世纪的电视机一样，在19世纪末曾风靡欧洲和美国，人们坐在自己家的客厅里用立体观片器欣赏世界各地的民俗和风景。但仔细观察这张照片，会发现左右图像并不是利用双镜头同时曝光而成，因为左右图像差别太大。应该是汤姆逊为了防止万一其中一张拍摄失败，而用两个镜头在不同时刻曝光而成。

A Chinese Portrait Artist

Hong Kong，1869，78×40.5 cm

European-style portrait painting was introduced into China long before the advent of photography. In the 17th century European oil painting had become very popular in southern China, particularly in cities such as Macau and Guangzhou, where Jesuit missionaries were active in training Chinese pupils to reproduce European religious paintings. In the imperial capital, Beijing, the Manchu emperors had also become fascinated by this novel western art, which, by the use of perspective, light and shade, resulted, in reproductions of horses or people that looked almost real. It did not take long for them to fully embrace European portrait painting and by the 18th century it had become an 'imperial tradition'. Thus Thomson was wrong to presume Chinese artists were simply trying to copy the artist George Chinnery, who resided in Macau. Even after the introduction of photography, many Chinese continued to prefer to have their portrait painted. This was partly because at the time photographs always came in black and white and in a small size, to have them enlarged was far too expensive. For those Chinese who did embrace photography, it was often because they did not have the patience to sit through a long portrait-painting session, they would have a photo taken, then ask a portrait painter to make a bigger reproduction of it in colour. At the time the Chinese word 'xiezhen', to 'transcribe the real', referred to both photography and portrait painting, suggesting there was little differentiation between the two.

Stereoscope first developed in North America, almost simultaneously with photography, it quickly became a popular form of entertainment throughout the late 19th century into the early 20th century. A stereoscope is composed of two pictures mounted next to each other, each picture is taken from a slightly different viewpoint that corresponds closely to the space between two eyes. The left picture represents what the left eye would see, and likewise for the right picture. The pictures are seen through a special lens: the pair of two-dimensional pictures merges into a single three-dimensional photograph.

天后庙乞丐僧侣

香港，1869年，41×40.5厘米

这是一个香港天后庙的僧侣。他的主要工作是协助信徒点香或者教授祈祷者一些基本礼仪。他是成千上万依附于寺庙但仍处于半饥饿状态的中国僧侣之一。

A Mendicant Priest

Hong Kong，1869，41×40.5 cm

Begging was one aspect of Chinese culture that Thomson was not comfortable with. He even referred to beggars as 'pests' and 'a source of great annoyance'. As for mendicants, he found them rather 'loathsome' and 'miserable', and called them 'half-starved hangers-on of monastic establishment'. According to him mendicants both cheated the poor and burdened them with taxes; they were simply society's parasites. In China, the majority of mendicants were attached to religious institutions. This individual was thought to have been attached to the famous Tin Hau Temple in the east of Hong Kong. In addition to begging for alms, his daily tasks involved lighting incense sticks and teaching short forms of prayers to worshippers.

九龙的贫困家庭

香港，1869年，40.5×51厘米

照片拍摄的是一家香港九龙家庭就餐时的情景。从照片中唯一站立的女主人可以看出当时中国的男尊女卑，桌上简单的饭食说明了这家的贫困。只有饭桌下等待残羹的三只小花猫为照片增添了些许生动。

A Cantonese Family of Kowloon

Hong Kong, 1869, 40.5×51 cm

While Thomson found the then British Crown Colony of Hong Kong comfortable and familiar, its Chinese population presented him with a curious way of life and character. He regarded the life of the poor in Hong Kong as not dissimilar to the life of the poor back in Britain: 'Poverty, insufficient and unwholesome food, a humid atmosphere and temperature over 90 degree in the shade, account in a great measure for the frequent visits of cholera and the black plague.' The Chinese, according to him, were superstitious and backward, and they 'stubbornly refuse sanitation as a body, or as individuals. But of this we have examples much nearer home, in the centres of congested population in our large towns.' This photograph shows a poor Chinese family living in Kowloon. Although Kowloon was handed to the British in 1860, it largely remained undeveloped until fairly recently and it was mainly occupied by an impoverished Chinese population.

维多利亚港湾赛舟

香港，1871年，67×40厘米

赛舟是英国传统的民间活动，英国统治香港后，也把这项活动带了过来。1849年，香港维多利亚赛舟会首次举办。照片拍摄的就是早期香港的一次赛舟活动，点点白帆衬托出了维多利亚港湾的美丽。1893年，维多利亚赛舟会易名为"皇家香港游艇会"，现在已经成为世界上最大规模的游艇会。

Regatta at Victoria Harbour

Hong Kong, 1871, 67×40 cm

It is thought rowing was the first organised water sport in Hong Kong. In October 1849 the first recorded yacht race took place in the then British Crown Colony under the auspices of the Victoria Regatta Club, and over the next 40 years the Club continued to hold races sporadically. In the meantime, a group of oarsmen also got together to form another club in North Point, known as the Hong Kong Boat Club. After the formation of Hong Kong Corinthian Sailing Club in 1890, which later became the Royal Hong Kong Yacht Club, the regatta became a regular and celebrated event in Hong Kong. Here we see Victoria Harbour, then one of the finest harbours in the world.

待客的轿夫

香港，1868-1871年，48×40.5厘米

在19世纪中期的香港，人力轿子是很受外国人欢迎的一种交通工具。汤姆逊在说明中写到：在宾馆，在码头，在各个主要路口，你到处可以看到这些被收拾得干干净净待客的人力轿子，轿夫们招呼着每一个刚刚到达港口的客人。照片以美丽的港湾为背景，一站一坐的轿夫，没有待客的焦灼，更多的是一份悠闲的心境。

Sedan Chair

Hong Kong, 1868–71, 48 × 40.5 cm

Until the introduction of the rickshaw in 1870, the sedan chair was the only form of public conveyance in Hong Kong. There were chair stands outside hotels, at major crossroads and by the wharfs. Public chairs were licensed and charged according to tariffs that were prominently displayed. The majority of chairs were kept fairly clean and in good condition, and the sturdy bearers would clamour for the favour of a client's regular patronage. Private chairs existed too, obvious markers of wealth and status. Even after the appearance of the rickshaw, the sedan chair continued to be one of the most important modes of transportation, since it was more suitable for the steep terrain of Hong Kong Island. In 1920 the number of sedan chairs peaked: about 1,215 registered ones were on the road. It was not until 1965 that the last sedan chair was reportedly abandoned.

香港动植物公园

香港，1871年，49×40厘米

地处太平山北坡香港植物公园的地段是曾作为香港总督的官邸。1864年，第一期设施开放给民众使用，1871年，公园全面开放，并正式定名为香港植物公园。当时的香港植物公园内以植物为主，照片中远处建筑是港督府和美丽的维多利亚港湾。从1876年起，公园开始饲养雀鸟及哺乳类动物，以供观赏。20世纪50年代后，公园扩建，主要辟作哺乳类及爬行类动物的居所，并在1975年易名为香港动植物公园。

View of Hong Kong Botanic Gardens from Albany

Hong Kong，1871，49×40 cm

The Victorian era in Europe was obsessed by the idea of cultivating exotic plants from distant lands. In the newly found Crown Colony, the idea of a public botanic garden emerged as early as 1848, but it was only in 1871 that the Hong Kong Botanic Gardens opened its doors to the public. The garden was located at Mid-levels on the northern slope of Victoria Peak, and was built on the site of Ping Tao Garden, which served as a temporary home for the former Governor Sir Henry Pottinger in 1841–2. In the early 1970s the Botanic Gardens underwent a significant expansion, and it began to house rare or endangered species of animals and birds for conservation and education purposes. It was renamed the Zoological and Botanical Gardens in 1975. The photo shows a view of Victoria Harbour at the time when the Garden was first opened. In the distance in front of the harbour stood St John's Cathedral and Headquarters House (now known as Flagstaff House). Both buildings had caused much controversy at the time for blemishing the colony's landscape, but they are now completely buried under a forest of skyscrapers.

伦核士街

香港，1869年，40×48.5厘米

伦核士街现为摆花街，位于香港中心位置，连接荷里活道和威灵顿街。1869年，爱丁堡公爵在去印度途中，短暂访问香港，成为第一个访问英国直辖殖民地的皇室成员。为了庆祝他的到来，香港街道装饰一新，这条大街就搭起了中国的牌楼，两边挤满了看热闹的人群和卫兵。

Lyndhurst Terrace

Hong Kong, 1869, 40×48.5 cm

This photograph was taken on Lyndhurst Street in the Central District of Hong Kong during H.R.H. the Duke of Edinburgh's brief visit in 1869. He was the first British Royal to visit the Crown Colony. To celebrate his short stopover in Hong Kong on his way to India, great efforts were made and the streets were full of festivities, elaborately decorated. Here is Lyndhurst Terrace decorated with a Chinese triumphal arch and other ornaments. On both side of the street are crowds of onlookers and some guards.

中国茶馆的阳台

香港，1868-1871年，40.5×41厘米

饮茶是南方人一个很重要的习惯。在19世纪后期，大量中国商人和劳动力来到香港，商业茶馆因此大量涌现。这些茶馆不仅供应茶水、点心等，还可供应鸦片，甚至性服务。图片上是一个中等规模的茶馆，有一个露天的阳台。人们来到阳台上，或站或坐，这也是当时中国人一种典型的社交活动。汤姆逊在同一地点还拍摄了中国人吸水烟的情景。

The Veranda of a Chinese Teahouse

Hong Kong, 1868–71, 40.5×41 cm

Tea drinking has been an important feature in southern China for a long time. In the second half of the 19th century, as an influx of Chinese merchants and labourers moved to Hong Kong, commercial teahouses flourished in response to the rising demand. There were various types of teahouses catering for different classes. Many of them not only served tea and snacks but also offered opium for smoking, as well as female attendants. This one is a typical middle-range teahouse with an open veranda.

南湾全景

澳门，1870年，49×40.5厘米

南湾为澳门的天然海湾之一，是澳门都市发展最早的地段。这张照片是从主教山山顶拍摄的。20世纪后，澳门政府在外港开展了大规模的填海改造工程，葡京酒店等地标性建筑出现，大大改变了南湾的原貌，我们只能从汤姆逊的照片中寻找南湾的记忆了。

View of the Praia Grande, Nam Van

Macau, 1870, 49×40.5 cm

Throughout the 19th century Praia Grande was the most fashionable address in Macau. It had captured the imagination of a number of artists and photographers and, from the 1820s onwards, a view of the Praia Grande was the souvenir of Macau par excellence. Both Chinnery and Lamqua were residents of Macau at the time, and the view of the Praia Grande was one of their favourite subjects. In 1844 Jules Itier, the head of the French trade commission in China, made the first photograph of this famous view in the form of a daguerreotype. In 1870, when Thomson took this photograph, he selected a view looking down on the Praia Grande from Penha Hill above Bishop's Bay. In the 20th century the area around Praia Grande underwent remarkable redevelopment, and it is no longer possible to see the famous view of picturesque Praia Grande except in old paintings, photos and postcards.

大三巴牌坊

澳门，1870年，41×49厘米

大三巴牌坊是澳门最具代表性的名胜古迹，为17世纪20年代年竣工的圣保罗大教堂的前壁，此教堂糅合了欧洲文艺复兴时期与东方的建筑风格而成，休现出东西艺术的交融。雕刻精细，巍峨壮观。教堂后于1835年惨遭大火焚毁，仅遗教堂前的68级石阶及花岗石建成的前壁，因貌似中国牌坊而得名。

The Ruins of St. Paul's

Macau, 1870, 41×49 cm

The ruinous church of St. Paul, which stands adjacent to the Mount Fortress was first constructed in 1580 by the Jesuit mission, and then rebuilt from 1602. The Baroque-style stone façade was completed in 1620's by a group of exiled Japanese Christians. The church was burned down in 1835. The surviving façade, with its four tiers of colonnades, is covered with carvings and statues that eloquently illustrate the early days of the Christian Church in Asia, and is regarded by many as a perfect fusion of western and eastern cultures. There are statues of the Virgin and saints, symbols of the Garden of Eden and the Crucifixion, angels and the Devil, a Chinese dragon and a Japanese chrysanthemum, a Portuguese sailing ship and pious warnings inscribed in Chinese.

琼州港的一个入口

海南，1870年，52×40.5厘米

琼州，即今天的海口，是当时海南岛主要港口。从1370年起，隶属于广东省，虽然在1858年的《天津条约》中列为对外通商口岸，但直到1872年才真正开放。这张照片拍摄的是琼州港的两个入口之一。当时的琼州还是一个城墙环绕的古城，比很多中国城市都干净、古朴。

A Fort at the Entrance to Qiongzhou (Haikou) Harbour

Hainan Island, 1870, 52×40.5 cm

Qiongzhou, known today as Haikou, was the main port of Hainan island off the southern coast of China. It became a part of China's Guangdong province in 1370. Although it was listed as one of the ports to be opened to foreign trade in the Treaty of Tianjin in 1858, it was not until 1872 that Qiongzhou was finally opened up and a British consul appointed to reside there. This photograph was taken two years before Qiongzhou became an open port; it shows one of the two forts at the entrance to the harbour. At the time of Thomson's visit Qiongzhou was a walled city, 'cleaner' and 'better kept' than most Chinese cities. It was surrounded by lavish countryside rich in agricultural produce.

古树和神祠

台湾，1868-1872年，40.5×43厘米

这是一幅体现了汤姆逊美学观念的摄影作品。在这幅作品中，路边巨大的古树和小巧的神祠生动地结合在一起，同时展现了人类和自然的联系。这个小小的神祠是当地小村庄的精神中心，它与巨大的古树根部相连，人们把贡品供奉在神祠中央的祭坛上，藉此找到了与大地的联系。

A Roadside Shrine

Taiwan，1868–72，40.5×43 cm

In Victorian times, Europeans had developed a taste for exotic 'scenes' – for landscapes as well as for people in faraway places. But Thomson was not interested in producing just 'lifeless charts of the mechanical proportions of nature'. A number of his landscape photographs of mainland China, Taiwan and South East Asia show the inherent atheistic qualities to his work as well as the human and spiritual dimensions behind each scene. In this photograph the enormous tree and small roadside shrine are brought alive by each other's presence, and they display the connection between man and nature. This small shrine not only represented the spiritual centre of the village, it also connected with the root of the gigantic old tree, and through it was joined to the earth. By making their offering to the altar in the centre of the shrine, people found a connection with mother earth.

平埔族人居所

台湾台南，1871年，47.5×39.5厘米

平埔族，是台湾原住民族群之一。汤姆逊在说明中详细描述了土著居民建造这些房子的过程：首先用竹子造好房屋结构，然后包上板条，更多的时候是包上用芦苇或用竹篾子编结的席子，接着取来粘土，掺入灰泥，再把墙体糊上，外层抹上用附近小山上到处可见的石灰岩石制成的白石灰，待其干透，就完工了。

Pepo Dwellings in Zuojhen (Zuozhen)

Tainan, Taiwan, 1871, 47.5×39.5 cm

'Pepo' is a generic term for the aborigines of Taiwan. There are at least 11 groups of aborigines whom Chinese call Pepohoan ('hoan' or 'fan' in Chinese means savages). Yet each group has its own distinct culture and tradition. The one Thomson came across near Tainan is generally thought to have been the Siraiya, which is the biggest group of Pepo in Taiwan, and many of them have intermarried with the local Chinese population. This photograph shows a typical Pepo dwelling in the late 19th century. According to Thomson, it was 'tolerably clean, well-arranged, and comfortable, and presents a striking uniformity of design in the different settlements throughout the island'. The structure of the dwelling was mainly made from bamboo. It is interesting to note that while the Chinese regarded the Siraiya as 'savages', Thomson found their dwellings were 'superior to those of the Chinese squatters, and the people themselves were better dressed'.

打狗海港全景

台湾高雄，1871年，40.5×41.5厘米

打狗（Takao，今高雄）开发得很早，是台湾历史最悠久的地方之一。这里最早是平埔族原住民（马卡道族）的居住地，因盛产竹子得名"Takao"（平埔族语，意为竹林），汉语音译为"打狗"，"打狗"是高雄最早的名称，日治时期改为"高雄"。打狗港最初于1680年代左右开港，属于浅水港，到了清朝末期亦对外开放成为通商口岸。

Takao Harbour

Kaoshiung, Taiwan，1871，40.5×41.5 cm

Takao, literaally meaning 'bamboo frost', was an ancient name for Kaoshiung. For centuries it served as a haven for lawless pirates and rebels. Although under the Dutch, and later on under the Chinese, it had developed into a prosperous fishing port, much of the landscape and coast remained unspoiled, with a great coral reef and 'luxuriant tropical trees'. With the Treaty of Peking (Beijing) in 1860, however, the Qing government was forced to open Takao as a port for foreign trade. A British consul was posted there, and a few houses and companies were set up by foreigners. But social unrest continued in Takao: robberies were a feature of life for the privileged British and other Europeans living there. Yet Thomson could see that 'in the hands of civilized foreign powers', Takao's social problems would soon disappear, but together with its natural beauty. This view of the harbour was taken from Takao Mountain, also known as Apes' Hill. The image shows the contrast between the already developed harbour and the uninhabited hill beyond.

后　记

我初次听到约翰·汤姆逊的名字是在伦敦维尔康姆图书馆的威廉·舒巴赫所主持的一场关于汤姆逊生平的讲座上。看到这些影像的第一眼，我就被深深地打动和吸引了。几个月之后，我在某个展览的开幕酒会上再次遇到了威廉，我先生不经意地问他汤姆逊的照片是否在中国展出过。威廉否定的回答令我们大吃一惊，同时也想到如果这些照片能够在中国展出该是一件多么有意义的事情。这已经是四年前的往事了。140年前，汤姆逊带着重重的三大箱玻璃底版回到伦敦，今天，这些19世纪中国的真实记录终于踏上了故乡的土地……

我想今天的观众可以从这些影像中获得不同的灵感：摄影爱好者会为汤姆逊在当时艰苦的环境下获得如此精美的影像所折服；设计师们可以欣赏到图中的服饰、发型、家具和建筑并观察到其细节；历史学家们可以从图中的市井与家庭看到人们生活的变迁。汤姆逊的作品中有大量的女性照片，这使我对他超越文化和语言障碍的沟通能力尤感赞叹。为了使这次展览达到更好的效果，我们的研究团队不遗余力地编写了信息丰富、引人入胜的说明，向大家介绍每张照片的时代背景。我衷心地希望观众们能够喜欢这次展览并在参观中有所收益，能够更加珍爱我们的传统与历史。

筹办这次展览完全是出自我的兴趣与热情，展览能够成功举办离不开许多朋友和赞助人的帮助。我在此感谢他们的热情鼓励和慷慨支持。

/姚詠蓓，嘉信文化

2009年4月

Postscript

My first introduction to the photographs of John Thomson was when I attended a talk by William Schupbach of the Wellcome Library in London, on Thomson's life and work. As soon as I saw these images, I was immediately fascinated by them. Some months later, we met again at a reception. My husband casually asked William whether Thomson's collection had ever been exhibited in China. We were both surprised when William said no, and added that it would be wonderful if they could be seen in China. That chance remark was made over 4 years ago. Today, nearly 140 years after John Thomson returned to London in 1872 with 3 heavy crates of glass negatives, this unique record of 19th century China has finally made the long trip home.

I hope today's audience and readers will enjoy and learn something new from these images and be inspired to cherish China's heritage and history. Photographic enthusiasts will marvel at the fine quality of his work, particularly given the arduous conditions that a 19th century photographer had to endure. Designers will admire the clothes, hairstyles, furniture and architecture and be able to study them in fine detail. Historians will revel in the street and domestic scenes, observing the day-to-day lives of people from a time past. I was especially surprised by the large number of images of women, showing Thomson's remarkable ability to communicate across language and cultural barriers. To enhance this exhibition our research team has done excellent work in producing informative and engaging captions, setting these images in the context of their time.

This exhibition has been a labour of love, but it would not have been possible without the ardent support of many friends and sponsors. I thank them all for their encouragement and generosity.

/ Betty Yao, Credential International Arts Management

April, 2009